Zha Methodology for Sustainability Mindset

"A framework to protect tomorrow's world, today"

Karki Ashokkumar

Made with ❤ on the Notion Press Platform

www.notionpress.co

Thank you to all the Zha Foundation advisory board members, all highly esteemed members of the board and club, for your great support and encouragement in doing greater innovative social work in the concept of sustainable development.

Dear Mr.Barath Subramanian, Mr.Udhayakumar, Ms.Prasanna Devi, and Mr.John Victor,

We are writing this letter to extend my heartfelt gratitude for your invaluable support in researching the ZHA Sustainability Mindset Curriculum. Your collective insights and diverse perspectives have been instrumental in deepening our understanding and advancing our work.

Barath, your analytical approach and attention to detail have provided a solid foundation for our study. Udhay, your innovative thinking and creative solutions have opened new avenues for exploration. Prasanna, your dedication and thoroughness have ensured our research remains comprehensive and accurate. John, your expertise and guidance have been crucial in navigating complex challenges.

Together, your contributions have significantly enriched our research, and for that, I am deeply grateful.

Thank you once again for your unwavering support and commitment.

Warm regards,

Karki Ashokkumar
Founder and Mentor,
ZHA Foundation
Charitable Trust,
Tamilnadu, India

Parimala Ashokkumar
President,
ZHA Foundation
Charitable Trust,
Tamilnadu, India

M Sabarinathan
Vice President,
ZHA Foundation
Charitable Trust,
Tamilnadu, India

Preface:

Karki Ashokkumar's experiences living in various countries such as Canada and the United States exposed him to different attitudes towards nature and the environment compared to those prevalent in India. He noticed that while sustainability policies were being advocated by the Indian government, there was a lack of understanding and commitment among the general population. The gap, particularly influenced by greed and selfishness, continued even in the era of technological advancement.

Need for Sustainability Mindset:

Recognizing the importance of addressing this gap, Karki Ashokkumar envisioned a framework for sustainability mindset enabling people to embrace sustainable practices. He understood that merely having policies in place was not sufficient; there was a need to educate and empower individuals to make sustainable choices in their daily lives. ZHA fostering Sustainability Mindset for People reinstates that change starts from you.

Global Professional Community Engagement:

To leverage expertise and perspectives from around the world, Karki Ashokkumar sought the involvement of the global professional community in leading the initiative. By inviting professionals from diverse backgrounds to become advisory members of the **Zha Sustainability Practitioners Club (ZSPC)**, he aimed to foster collaboration and knowledge sharing on sustainable practices.

ZHA Foundation Ethics:

Drawing from his upbringing in the villages and suburbs of Tamil Nadu, India, Karki Ashokkumar emphasized the importance of social responsibility, commitment, courage, openness and integrity as foundational ethics. He recognized the need to combat the prevalent mindset of greed and selfishness by promoting values that prioritize the well-being of society and the environment.

Examples:

1. *Cross-Cultural Observations:* Karki Ashokkumar's experiences living in different countries allowed him to observe varying attitudes towards sustainability and environmental stewardship. For instance, he noticed a stronger culture of recycling and conservation in Canada compared to India.

2. *Government Policies vs. Public Understanding:* Despite the Indian government's efforts to promote sustainability policies, Karki Ashokkumar observed a disconnect

between policy implementation and public understanding. For example, while regulations might be in place to reduce plastic waste, public awareness and compliance could be lacking.

3. *Global Professional Community Engagement:* Karki Ashokkumar's invitation for professionals from around the world to join the ZSPC as advisory members demonstrates his commitment to leveraging diverse expertise. For instance, professionals from the US might bring insights on sustainable business practices, while those from Canada might offer perspectives on environmental conservation.
4. *Foundation Ethics in Action:* Karki Ashokkumar's emphasis on social equality and responsibility can be reflected in initiatives undertaken by the Zha Foundation Charitable Trust. For example, the trust might prioritize projects that benefit marginalized communities or promote sustainable livelihoods in rural areas.

Table of Contents

CHAPTER 1:
Zha Foundations' Journey

ZHA Foundation Vision and Mission:

Vision:

To build a better future for the next generations, the ZHA Foundation is dedicated to the dual purpose of nurturing a sustainable mindset and conserving the natural resources of our planet.

Mission:

The Zha Foundation, strives to cultivate a global community committed to fostering a sustainable mindset. We aim to transcend the negative impacts of unchecked greed and jealousy, recognizing their potential harm to nations and the planet's delicate balance. Collaborating with professionals and business leaders, our foundation advocates for a sustainable future, steering away from conflicts and promoting unity through three guiding principles for our Zha members: No politics-based discussions, no discussions based on religion or caste, and a commitment to refrain from speaking negatively about fellow members.

Sustainable development is imperative for a better tomorrow, balancing present needs without jeopardizing the well-being of future generations. The survival of our societies and shared planet hinges on fostering a sustainable mindset. The Sustainable Development Goals (SDGs), comprising seventeen interconnected objectives, serve as a "shared blueprint for peace and prosperity for people and the planet, now and into the future".

Role of ZHA in promoting sustainability

Sustainability for people refers to the concept or methodology of ensuring that human societies can thrive and prosper in harmony with the environment, both now and in the future. It encompasses various dimensions, including social, economic, and environmental aspects, with the overarching goal of meeting the needs of the present generation without compromising the requirements of future generations.

Expanding a sustainability development club like Zha Foundation to all countries allows for a global impact by addressing diverse environmental and social challenges. It enables the sharing of resources, knowledge, and best practices, fostering a collaborative approach towards sustainable development on a broader scale. Additionally, the interconnected nature of global issues emphasizes the need for widespread participation to create a more sustainable and resilient world.

Root causes of Unsustainable Human Life:

Unsustainable lifestyles for humans can be attributed to several interconnected factors:

1. **Excessive Mobile Phone Usage:** Children and parents are increasingly spending a significant amount of time on mobile phones, which has led to a decline in physical activity, reading habits, and social interaction.
2. **Video Game Overuse :** Children, in particular, are devoting excessive hours to video games, often at the expense of participating in sports and cultivating a love for reading.
3. **Erosion of Social Trust :** Reduced face-to-face interactions between people due to digital distractions are contributing to a decline in trust and interpersonal relationships, raising concerns about the quality of our social connections.

4. **Over Consumption and Materialism :** The pursuit of excessive material possessions and consumption of resources beyond what is necessary for a comfortable and fulfilling life can lead to unsustainable lifestyles.

5. **Resource Depletion :** Over-exploitation of natural resources, including fossil fuels, minerals, and freshwater, can lead to their depletion and contribute to environmental degradation.

6. **Waste Generation :** Inefficient resource use and improper waste disposal contribute to pollution, landfill accumulation, and the release of harmful substances into the environment.

7. **High Energy Consumption :** Reliance on energy-intensive practices, such as excessive use of electricity, heating, and transportation, can lead to increased greenhouse gas emissions and environmental strain.

8. **Transportation and Commuting Habits :** Reliance on personal vehicles for transportation, particularly in areas lacking efficient public transit, can contribute to air pollution, congestion, and fossil fuel consumption.

9. **Food Production and Consumption :** Unsustainable agricultural practices, including monoculture farming, excessive use of chemical inputs, and long-distance transportation of food, can lead to environmental degradation and food security challenges.

10. **Deforestation and Habitat Destruction :** Clearing land for agriculture, urbanization, and infrastructure development can lead to loss of biodiversity, disruption of ecosystems, and reduced carbon sequestration.

11. **Celebrating Life's Victories :** We often fail to celebrate others achievements, as well as our own.

12. **Neglecting Sympathy :** We often neglect to share our condolences for other's losses

13. **Overfishing and Marine Degradation :** Unsustainable fishing practices, including overfishing and destructive fishing methods, can deplete fish stocks and harm marine ecosystems.

14. **Lack of Sustainable Infrastructure :** Inadequate urban planning, incompetent building designs, and outdated infrastructure can contribute to resource inefficiency and environmental strain.

15. **Consumer Behavior and Choices :** Choices made by consumers, such as purchasing non-sustainable products, can drive the demand for resource-intensive and environmentally harmful goods and services.

16. **Lack of Environmental Awareness and Education :** Insufficient knowledge and understanding of the environmental impacts of certain behaviors can lead to unintentional unsustainable practices.

17. **Policy and Regulatory Frameworks :** Weak or inadequate environmental policies, lack of enforcement, and subsidies that incentivize unsustainable practices can contribute to unsustainable lifestyles.

Addressing unsustainable lifestyles requires a multi-faceted approach, including education, policy changes, technological innovation, and shifts in cultural and societal norms. Encouraging sustainable practices, promoting responsible consumption, and adopting eco-friendly technologies are all important steps towards a more sustainable future.

Thus, since 2017 Zha Foundation's journey towards recognizing the importance of a sustainability mindset has unfolded through a series of observations, experiences, and realizations over the past decade. Let's delve into how the foundation came to understand the critical need for a sustainability mindset to ensure a sustainable future, especially in the face of widespread issues such as natural calamities, diseases, extinctions, suicides, and wars, all of which stem from the lack of adherence to sustainability principles.

Initial Observations:

1. Over the past ten years, the Zha Foundation witnessed an alarming increase in environmental degradation, social injustices, and economic disparities worldwide. They have observed the rising temperatures, extreme weather events, deforestation, pollution, and loss of biodiversity, all of which are symptoms of an unsustainable world. Additionally, they noted the disproportionate impact of these issues on vulnerable communities, exacerbating poverty, inequality, and social unrest.

Connecting the Dots:

2. As the Zha Foundation continued its work and research, they began to connect the dots between these various problems and their underlying causes. They have realized that many challenges in society faced today are interconnected and stem from a common root: the lack of consideration for long-term sustainability in decision-making processes. Whether it's exploitation of natural resources, overconsumption, or disregard for social and environmental impacts, unsustainable practices have far-reaching consequences that threaten the well-being of people and the planet.

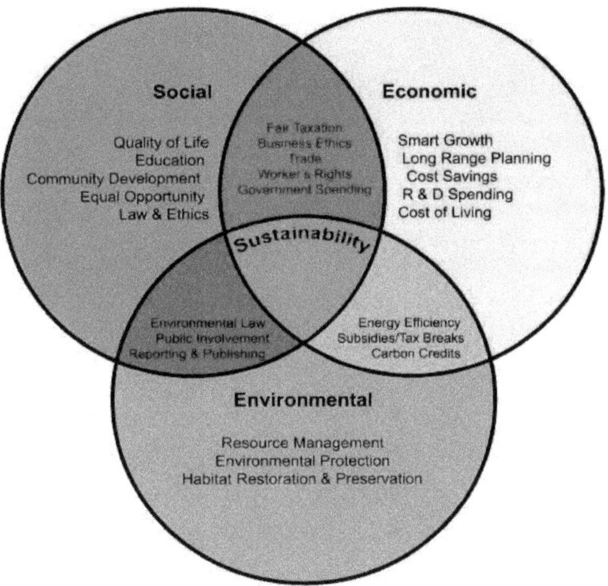

Learning from Consequences:

3. The foundation paid close attention to the consequences of unsustainable behavior, as evidenced by natural calamities, disease outbreaks, species extinctions, mental health crises, and conflicts. These events serve as stark reminders of the interconnectedness of human activities and the environment, highlighting the need for a fundamental shift in mindset to prioritize sustainability. They have witnessed the devastating effects of climate change on communities, the loss of livelihoods due to environmental degradation, and the toll of resource scarcity on human health and security.

Identifying Root Causes:

4. Through research, collaboration, and dialogue with experts and stakeholders, the Zha Foundation delved deeper into understanding the root causes of unsustainable practices and mindset. They have identified factors such as short-term thinking, profit maximization, lack of awareness, institutional inertia, and systemic inequalities as barriers to achieving sustainability. Recognizing these barriers is crucial for devising effective strategies to promote a sustainability mindset and drive transformative change.

Chapter 2:

Why Cultivating a Sustainability Mindset among People?

The need for a sustainability mindset

The need for a sustainability mindset among people is paramount in addressing the complex and interconnected challenges facing our planet today. Here are several key reasons why fostering a sustainability mindset is crucial:

Environmental Preservation:

1. A sustainability mindset recognizes the finite nature of our planet's resources and the importance of preserving natural ecosystems. By embracing sustainable practices such as reducing waste, conserving energy and water, and protecting biodiversity, individuals can minimize their ecological footprint and contribute to environmental sustainability.

Climate Change Mitigation:

2. Climate change poses one of the most significant threats to human civilization, with far-reaching impacts on weather patterns, sea levels, ecosystems, and human health. Adopting a sustainability mindset involves taking action to reduce greenhouse gas emissions, transition to renewable energy sources, and adapting to the changing climate to mitigate its adverse effects.

Resource Conservation:

3. Unsustainable consumption patterns and resource depletion are degrading ecosystems, threatening biodiversity, and exacerbating environmental degradation. A sustainability mindset promotes responsible resource management, circular economy principles, and efficient use of resources to ensure their availability for future generations.

Social Equity and Justice:

4. Sustainability is inherently linked to social equity and justice, as it seeks to ensure that all people, regardless of their background or circumstances, have access to basic needs such as clean water, nutritious food, and adequate shelter. Fostering a sustainability mindset involves addressing systemic inequalities, promoting inclusive development, and advocating for social justice and human rights.

Economic Resilience:

5. Embracing sustainability principles can enhance economic resilience by promoting innovation, resource efficiency, and long-term prosperity. Businesses that prioritize sustainability are better positioned to adapt to changing market dynamics, reduce operational costs, and mitigate risks associated with environmental and social disruptions.

Interconnectedness of Systems:

6. A sustainability mindset recognizes the interconnectedness of environmental, social, and economic systems and the complex relationships between them. By understanding these interdependencies, individuals can make informed decisions that consider the broader impacts of their actions on people, the planet, and future generations.

Empowerment and Engagement:

7. Fostering a sustainability mindset empowers individuals to take action and make positive changes in their communities and beyond. By raising awareness, promoting education, and encouraging civic engagement, individuals can become agents of change and contribute to building a more sustainable and resilient world.

How to cultivate a sustainability mindset among people

Cultivating a sustainability mindset involves adopting a holistic perspective that considers the interconnectedness of environmental, social, and economic systems and integrates sustainability principles into daily life decisions and actions. Hence, regular social work practices based on various solutions, enable a sustainability mindset in every individual.

Holistic Perspective

A sustainability mindset requires understanding that environmental, social, and economic systems are deeply interconnected. This means recognizing how actions in one area can have wide-ranging impacts on others. For example, environmental degradation can lead to social inequalities and economic challenges. A holistic perspective encourages individuals to think broadly about the consequences of their actions and to strive for solutions that balance the needs of these three pillars of sustainability.]

Integration into Daily Life

Integrating sustainability principles into daily life involves making conscious choices that reflect a commitment to sustainability. This can include reducing waste, conserving energy, supporting sustainable products and businesses, and advocating for policies that promote environmental and social well-being. By embedding these principles into everyday decisions and actions, individuals can contribute to a more sustainable world.

Here are steps to help individuals cultivate a sustainability mindset:

Educate Yourself:

1. Start by learning about sustainability concepts, challenges, and solutions through books, articles, documentaries, online courses, and reputable sources. Develop an understanding of environmental issues, social justice, resource management, and sustainable development goals.

Raise Awareness:

2. Spread awareness about sustainability issues and their impacts on people and the planet within your community, workplace, and social networks. Engage in conversations, share information, and encourage others to take action and make sustainable choices in their daily lives.

Practice Mindfulness:

3. Cultivate mindfulness and awareness of your consumption patterns, lifestyle choices, and environmental impact. Consider the environmental and social implications of your actions, purchases, and habits, and strive to minimize waste, conserve resources, and reduce your ecological footprint.

Set Goals:

4. Set personal sustainability goals to guide your actions and behaviors. Identify areas where you can make positive changes, such as reducing energy consumption, minimizing waste, adopting plant-based diets, supporting sustainable businesses, or volunteering for environmental causes.

Lead by Example:

5. Be a role model for sustainability by integrating eco-friendly practices into your life and inspiring others to follow suit. Demonstrate sustainable behaviors such as

recycling, using reusable products, conserving water, biking or using public transportation, and supporting ethical and eco-conscious brands.

Get Involved:

6. Get involved in sustainability initiatives, community projects, and environmental organizations that align with your values and interests. Volunteer for clean-up events, tree plantings, environmental advocacy campaigns, or local sustainability groups to make a positive impact in your community.

Advocate for Change:

7. Advocate for policies, regulations, and practices that promote sustainability at the local, national, and global levels. Write to elected officials, participate in public consultations, support environmental petitions, and vote for candidates who prioritize environmental and social issues.

Continue Learning and Evolving:

8. Stay informed and continue learning about new developments, innovations, and best practices in sustainability. Be open to feedback, reflection, and self-improvement, and adapt your behaviors and choices based on new knowledge and insights.

By following these steps and actively cultivating a sustainability mindset, individuals can contribute to building a more sustainable and resilient world for current and future generations. Remember that even small actions can make a meaningful difference when multiplied by collective efforts and shared commitment to sustainability.

Role of Educational Institutions in fostering a sustainability mindset among students

The role of educational institutions among students is instrumental in shaping the attitudes, values, and behaviors of future generations towards environmental stewardship, social responsibility, and economic resilience. Hence, institutions need to integrate with the **ZHA Sustainability Process and Curriculum (ZSPC)** to ensure that students practice a systematic approach to sustainability.

Educational institutions have a pivotal role in shaping the future by instilling a sustainability mindset in students. By integrating with the ZHA Sustainability Process and Curriculum (ZSPC), institutions can provide a structured and effective approach to teaching sustainability. This integration ensures that students not only learn about sustainability but also practice it systematically, preparing them to be responsible, informed, and proactive stewards of the environment, society, and economy.

Role of Educational Institutions

Educational institutions play a critical role in developing a sustainability mindset by:

1. **Shaping Attitudes**: Schools and universities influence students' perspectives on the importance of sustainability. Through exposure to sustainability concepts, students develop positive attitudes towards environmental stewardship, social responsibility, and economic resilience.
2. **Instilling Values**: Educational settings are where core values are nurtured. By emphasizing values such as equity, justice, and respect for nature, institutions foster a generation that prioritizes sustainability in their personal and professional lives.
3. **Guiding Behaviors**: Practical applications of sustainability principles in educational contexts encourage

students to adopt sustainable behaviors. This includes initiatives like recycling programs, energy conservation measures, and community service projects.

Importance of Integrating & Starting with ZSPC

The ZHA Sustainability Practitioners Club, Process and Curriculum (ZSPC) is a comprehensive framework designed to systematically embed sustainability into education. Integrating with ZSPC ensures that institutions can:

1. **Provide Structured Learning**: ZSPC offers a well-defined curriculum that covers all aspects of sustainability, ensuring that students receive a thorough education on the topic.
2. **Promote Systematic Processes**: The process-oriented approach of ZSPC helps in systematically implementing sustainability practices in schools, making sustainability an integral part of the institution's culture.
3. **Encourage Active Participation**: Through project-based learning and community engagement activities outlined in ZSPC, students actively participate in sustainability initiatives, reinforcing their learning through practical experience.
4. **Facilitate Continuous Improvement**: ZSPC includes mechanisms for regular assessment and feedback, allowing institutions to continually refine their sustainability practices and curriculum to better meet educational goals and evolving sustainability challenges.

Practical Steps for Integration

1. **Curriculum Development**: Align existing curricula with ZSPC guidelines to ensure comprehensive coverage of sustainability topics across various subjects.

2. **Teacher Training**: Provide professional development for educators to effectively deliver sustainability education and implement ZSPC processes.
3. **Student Engagement**: Create opportunities for students to engage in sustainability projects, such as eco-clubs, sustainability-themed competitions, and community service initiatives.
4. **Partnerships**: Collaborate with local communities, businesses, and environmental organizations to enhance the practical application of sustainability concepts learned in the classroom.
5. **Evaluation and Feedback**: Establish systems to regularly evaluate the effectiveness of sustainability education and gather feedback from students and staff to continuously improve the program.

Here's how education can enable the next generation with a sustainability mindset:

Environmental Literacy:

1. Education provides students with knowledge and understanding of environmental issues, ecosystems, and the interconnections between human activities and the natural world. By integrating environmental education into school curricula, students learn about sustainability concepts, ecological principles, and the importance of biodiversity conservation, empowering them to become informed and responsible environmental stewards.

Critical Thinking and Problem-Solving:

2. Education fosters critical thinking skills and encourages students to analyze complex sustainability challenges, evaluate evidence, and develop innovative solutions. Through inquiry-based learning, hands-on activities, and project-based assignments, students learn to identify

environmental problems, explore root causes, and propose sustainable alternatives, preparing them to address real-world sustainability issues in their communities and beyond.

Systems Thinking:

3. Education promotes systems thinking, which involves understanding the interconnectedness of environmental, social, and economic systems and the dynamic relationships between them. By examining the complex interactions between human activities and the environment, students gain insights into the systemic drivers of sustainability challenges and learn to consider the broader impacts of their actions on people and the planet.

Values and Ethics:

4. Education instills values such as empathy, respect, and responsibility for the well-being of others and the environment. By incorporating ethics and moral reasoning into the curriculum, students develop a strong sense of environmental and social justice and learn to make ethical decisions that prioritize the common good and future generations' needs over short-term gains.

Empowerment and Agency:

5. Education empowers students to take action and make positive changes in their communities and the world. By providing opportunities for experiential learning, service-learning projects, and civic engagement activities, education enables students to apply their knowledge and skills to address sustainability challenges, advocate for social and environmental justice, and become agents of change in their schools and beyond.

Lifelong Learning and Adaptability:

6. Education fosters a culture of lifelong learning and adaptability, equipping students with the resilience and agility needed to navigate a rapidly changing world. By cultivating curiosity, creativity, and a growth mindset, education enables students to continuously seek new information, explore diverse perspectives, and adapt to evolving sustainability challenges and opportunities throughout their lives.

In summary, education plays a crucial role in fostering a sustainability mindset among students by providing environmental literacy, critical thinking skills, system thinking abilities, ethical values, empowerment, and adaptability. By enabling the next generation with a sustainability mindset, education prepares students to become informed, engaged, and responsible global citizens who can contribute to building a more sustainable and resilient future for all.

CHAPTER 3:

Introduction to ZHA Sustainability Practitioners Club - A Methodology:

Author Karki Ashokkumar, the founder of the Zha Sustainability Practitioners Club (ZSPC), is aligning the Zha Framework for Sustainability Mindset for the purpose of enabling a set up with pathway(Methodology) for club members to benchmark its future versions based on the needs of the world in benefiting the planet, people, peace, and nature conservation. Here's how a ZHA framework version 1.0, drives the ZSPC club through a curriculum:

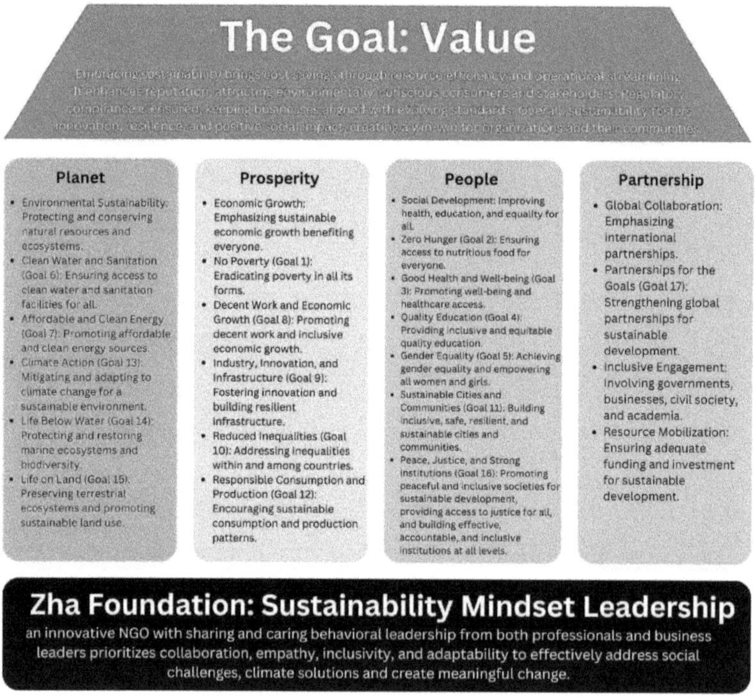

The Goal: Value

Planet

- Environmental Sustainability: Protecting and conserving natural resources and ecosystems.
- Clean Water and Sanitation (Goal 6): Ensuring access to clean water and sanitation facilities for all.
- Affordable and Clean Energy (Goal 7): Promoting affordable and clean energy sources.
- Climate Action (Goal 13): Mitigating and adapting to climate change for a sustainable environment.
- Life Below Water (Goal 14): Protecting and restoring marine ecosystems and biodiversity.
- Life on Land (Goal 15): Preserving terrestrial ecosystems and promoting sustainable land use.

Prosperity

- Economic Growth: Emphasizing sustainable economic growth benefiting everyone.
- No Poverty (Goal 1): Eradicating poverty in all its forms.
- Decent Work and Economic Growth (Goal 8): Promoting decent work and inclusive economic growth.
- Industry, Innovation, and Infrastructure (Goal 9): Fostering innovation and building resilient infrastructure.
- Reduced Inequalities (Goal 10): Addressing inequalities within and among countries.
- Responsible Consumption and Production (Goal 12): Encouraging sustainable consumption and production patterns.

People

- Social Development: Improving health, education, and equality for all.
- Zero Hunger (Goal 2): Ensuring access to nutritious food for everyone.
- Good Health and Well-being (Goal 3): Promoting well-being and healthcare access.
- Quality Education (Goal 4): Providing inclusive and equitable quality education.
- Gender Equality (Goal 5): Achieving gender equality and empowering all women and girls.
- Sustainable Cities and Communities (Goal 11): Building inclusive, safe, resilient, and sustainable cities and communities.
- Peace, Justice, and Strong Institutions (Goal 16): Promoting peaceful and inclusive societies for sustainable development, providing access to justice for all, and building effective, accountable, and inclusive institutions at all levels.

Partnership

- Global Collaboration: Emphasizing international partnerships.
- Partnerships for the Goals (Goal 17): Strengthening global partnerships for sustainable development.
- Inclusive Engagement: Involving governments, businesses, civil society, and academia.
- Resource Mobilization: Ensuring adequate funding and investment for sustainable development.

Zha Foundation: Sustainability Mindset Leadership

an innovative NGO with sharing and caring behavioral leadership from both professionals and business leaders prioritizes collaboration, empathy, inclusivity, and adaptability to effectively address social challenges, climate solutions and create meaningful change.

1. Alignment with Zha Framework: By integrating the pillars into the club's mission, vision, and activities, Karki ensures that club members are guided by principles that promote sustainability, social responsibility, and collaboration.
2. Pathway for Benchmarking: The club involves in regularly assessing the club's performance in advancing sustainability goals, promoting social responsibility, and fostering collaboration among members and stakeholders.
3. Focus on Benefitting the World: The club aims to address pressing sustainability challenges, promote social justice and equity, and contribute to the conservation of natural resources and biodiversity.

Enabling Social Responsibility through ZHA Principles for Sustainable Mindset

Karki recognizes the importance of instilling these principles from childhood and advocates for the implementation of ZSPC in every school and college. Here's how:

1. Early Exposure to Principles: By introducing the Zha Principles at a young age through the ZSPC curriculum, Karki aims to cultivate a sense of social and ethical responsibility and environmental stewardship from childhood. This early exposure helps students develop sustainable habits and moral values that they carry into adulthood and pass on to society.
2. Measuring Principle Activation: Karki emphasizes the significance of measuring the sustainability principles while students participate in ZSPC curriculum activities. This involves assessing students' comprehension, adoption, and application of the Zha Principles in their daily lives, projects, and initiatives within the club.

Lastly, ZHA Foundation envisions successful professionals leading ZSPC activities from anywhere, including remotely, to spread knowledge and build a research and development culture within the club's community. Here's how this benefits the club:

1. Knowledge Sharing: Engaging successful professionals as torch bearers in ZSPC activities facilitates knowledge sharing, mentorship, and networking opportunities for club members. Professionals synergize diverse expertise, perspectives, and experiences to the club, enriching its learning environment and fostering innovation.
2. Research and Development Culture: By encouraging professionals to lead ZSPC activities, ZHA promotes a unique blend of culture of research and development (R&D) within the club. This involves encouraging members to explore new ideas, experiment with innovative solutions, and collaborate on projects that address sustainability challenges and opportunities.

Overall, by aligning with the Zha Framework, instilling sustainability principles from childhood, and engaging successful professionals as leaders, Author Karki aims to empower ZSPC members to become effective agents of change for a more sustainable and equitable world.

How ethical values of ZHA Foundation Aligns its ZSPC Members with the Vision of "Sustainability for People"

Foundational ethics values can effectively align its ZSPC members with the vision of enabling sustainability mindset among people.

Let's explore how each of these values contributes to this alignment:

1. Social Responsibility:

   ZSPC members who embody social responsibility understand their role in contributing to the well-being of society and the environment. They prioritize sustainability initiatives that benefit communities and ecosystems, demonstrating empathy and accountability for their actions

2. Commitment:

   Commitment ensures that ZSPC members remain dedicated to the vision and goals of enabling sustainability mindset. They are willing to invest time, effort, and resources into sustainability initiatives, persevering through challenges and setbacks to achieve meaningful impact.

3. Courage:

   Courage empowers ZSPC members to challenge the status quo and advocate for change in support of sustainability. They are willing to take bold actions, speak out against unsustainable practices, and champion innovative solutions, even in the face of opposition or resistance.

4. Openness:

   Openness fosters a culture of collaboration, learning, and adaptation within the ZSPC community. Members who embrace openness are receptive to diverse perspectives, ideas, and feedback, recognizing the value of dialogue and co-creation in driving sustainable change.

5. Integrity:

   Integrity ensures that ZSPC members act with honesty, transparency, and ethical conduct in all their endeavors. They uphold high standards of integrity in their interactions with stakeholders, making decisions that prioritize the common good and long-term sustainability.

By embodying these foundational ethics, ZSPC members can effectively align with the vision of enabling sustainability mindset among people in the following ways:

- Leading by Example: ZSPC members who demonstrate foundational ethics serve as role models for others, inspiring them to adopt sustainable behaviors and attitudes.
- Building Trust and Credibility: Upholding these values enhances the trust and credibility of the ZSPC within communities and among stakeholders. People are more likely to engage with and support sustainability initiatives led by individuals and organizations known for their ethical conduct and genuine commitment.
- Fostering Collaboration and Partnership: Values such as openness and integrity foster collaboration and partnership among ZSPC members and with external stakeholders. By working together with shared values and goals, they can leverage collective expertise and resources to amplify their impact and reach.
- Driving Innovation and Resilience: Courage and commitment empower ZSPC members to innovate, experiment, and adapt in response to evolving sustainability challenges. By embracing change with integrity and courage, they can drive continuous improvement and resilience in their sustainability efforts.

In summary, the context highlights Karki Ashokkumar's vision for promoting sustainability mindset, drawing on his cross-cultural experiences and emphasizing foundational ethics to address challenges in fostering sustainable behavior among the public.

Chapter 4:

Background of ZHA Sustainability Mindset Framework

In the wake of global challenges such as climate change, resource depletion, and environmental degradation, the importance of sustainability has become increasingly evident. Sustainability is not merely a buzzword; it is a fundamental principle that guides actions toward preserving our planet's health and ensuring the well-being of current and future generations. However, despite growing awareness, there remain significant gaps in the sustainability mindset that hinder progress toward a truly sustainable world.

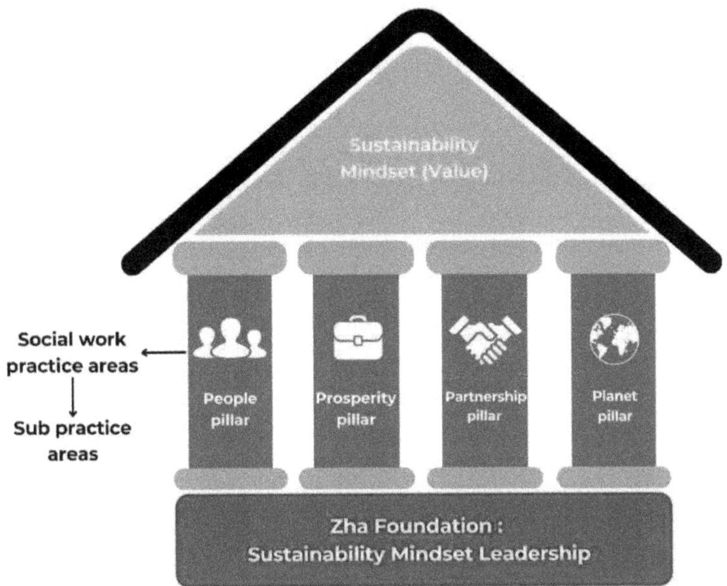

The above ZHA Sustainability Mindset Framework Version 2.0 comprises of four pillars:

People, Partnerships, Planet, and Prosperity. Each pillar includes specific social work practices, which are further divided into sub-practice areas. These sub-practice areas are used to assess the maturity of practitioners within the ZHA Sustainability Practitioners Club. The goal is that membership in the ZHA Sustainability Club for at least five years cultivates a sustainability mindset in its members. Each social work practice area generates a curriculum topic.

This curriculum enables ZHA Club members to participate in various activities practically and effectively, contributing to national efforts and resource conservation. Background of the Zha Sustainability Mindset Framework :

1. ZHA Sustainability Mindset Framework: -

Four Pillars of ZHA Sustainability Mindset Framework: -

People: Focuses on human and social aspects. -

Partnerships: Emphasizes collaboration and cooperative efforts.

Planet: Concerns environmental sustainability and conservation.

Prosperity: Relates to economic growth and sustainable development.

2. Social Work Practices:- Each pillar contains specific practices aimed at promoting sustainability. These practices are further divided into sub-practice areas to address specific aspects of sustainability.

3. Assessment of Practitioners: - The sub-practice areas are used as criteria to evaluate the maturity and progress of practitioners in the ZHA Sustainability Practitioners Club. - Practitioners' engagement and development in these areas are monitored to ensure they are adopting and embodying sustainable practices.

4. Outcome of Membership: - Sustained membership (at least five years) in the ZHA Sustainability Club is designed to instill a deep-rooted sustainability mindset in members. - This long-term involvement ensures that members not only understand but also practice sustainability principles in their daily lives.

5. Curriculum and Activities:- Each social work practice area is linked to a specific curriculum topic. The curriculum provides practical and effective activities for members to engage in. These activities are designed to help members contribute to broader national sustainability efforts and conserve resources.

Thus, The ZHA Sustainability Mindset Framework is a comprehensive approach that integrates social, environmental, and economic aspects of sustainability. Through structured practices and long-term engagement, it aims to cultivate a deeply ingrained sustainability mindset in its members. The curriculum and activities provided ensure practical application and active participation in sustainability initiatives.

Using ZSPC Methodology as "Common Man - Community of Practice" along with Curriculum for Students

The Zha Sustainability Practitioners Club is otherwise called the Common Man - Community of Practices (COPs) which aims to cultivate a sustainability mindset among individuals globally. Mentored by Zha Foundation's global board members, the COPs focus on monthly forums to educate, discuss, and inspire action toward sustainable practices. The goals include raising awareness, sharing best practices, and cultivating a global network committed to sustainability. Benefits include knowledge exchange, collaborative initiatives, and empowering individuals to contribute to a more sustainable world.

Our ZSPC has various COPs for every members from any country, focusing on delivering sessions, resolution outcome and innovating initiatives based on the following agendas

1. **Education and Awareness: Zha's** COPs provide a platform for common people to gain knowledge about climate change and sustainability, fostering a deeper understanding of their significance.

2. **Local Impact :** By engaging common individuals, the COPs empower local communities to take action, contributing collectively to global sustainability efforts.

3. **Behavioral Change :** The COPs aim to influence daily habits and practices, encouraging sustainable choices among participants who may not initially grasp the importance of climate change.

4. **Community Empowerment:** Through mentorship and collaboration, the COPs empower individuals to become advocates for sustainability within their communities, creating a ripple effect of positive change.

5. **Global Network :** The COPs connect people from diverse backgrounds, fostering a sense of global responsibility and illustrating how individual actions collectively impact the planet.

6. **Alignment with UN Goals :** Zha's COPs directly align with the United Nations' sustainability goals, offering a grassroots approach of achieving broader global objectives.

7. **Inclusive Participation :** By targeting common people, the COPs ensure inclusivity, engaging a wider demographic and avoiding the exclusion of those unfamiliar with the language or concepts of sustainability.

8. **Monthly Forums :**Regular forums provide a consistent platform for ongoing dialogue and learning, reinforcing the importance of sustainability over time and making it a part of participants' ongoing consciousness.

9. **Practical Solutions :** The COPs focus on practical, achievable solutions that common people can implement in their daily lives, making sustainability more accessible and less abstract.

10. **Adaptation and Resilience :** Educating common people through COPs helps communities adapt to changing environmental conditions and develop resilience against the impacts of climate change.

To wrap up, Zha's Common Man COPs play a crucial role in bridging the gap between the abstract concepts of climate change and sustainability goals and the practical actions of everyday individuals. Creating a more sustainable and informed global society with a sustainability mindset to protect nature, environment and peace.

Chapter 5:

What are the Pillars of Sustainability Framework?

Recognizing the critical role education plays in shaping a sustainable future, we propose an innovative sustainability curriculum designed to empower our young citizens. This curriculum is structured around four robust pillars—4-P's Planet, Prosperity, People and Partnerships—each meticulously crafted to address the diverse challenges specific to our state and beyond.

These pillars are designed not merely as educational content but as a dynamic framework for action. This proposal outlines a comprehensive strategy to integrate these pillars into the Tamil Nadu educational system, transforming theoretical knowledge into practical, impactful actions. By embedding these sustainability pillars in our curriculum, we aim to cultivate environmentally conscious leaders, innovators, and citizens who are equipped to make informed decisions and lead initiatives that will drive our state towards a greener and more sustainable future.

The necessity for such an educational overhaul has never been more urgent. As India continues to grow economically and industrially, the imperative to balance this growth with environmental stewardship is paramount. Through this method, we seek not only to educate but also to inspire our students, instilling in them the values of ecological and social responsibility from young ages. We are confident that the implementation of this curriculum will mark a significant step forward in our collective efforts to address environmental challenges, fostering a culture of sustainability that permeates every level of our society.

Detailed exploration of the 4-Pillars: Planet, Prosperity, People, and Partnerships

Planet

Planet pillar emphasizes the protection and sustainability of our natural environment, ensuring that future generations have access to natural resources and a healthy planet. It involves actions aimed at preserving ecosystems, managing natural resources responsibly, and mitigating the effects of climate change.

Clean Water and Sanitation

Ensure availability and sustainable management of water and sanitation for all.

Focuses on providing universal access to safe and affordable drinking water for everyone, improving sanitation and hygiene facilities, and enhancing water quality by reducing pollution, eliminating dumping, and minimizing the release of hazardous chemicals. It also stresses the importance of efficient water usage and sustainable water management practices to alleviate water scarcity.

- Water Conservation Workshops: Schools and colleges can host workshops to educate students on water conservation techniques, such as fixing leaks, using water-efficient fixtures, and harvesting rainwater.
- Water Quality Monitoring Projects: Students can engage in local projects to monitor and report on the water quality of nearby rivers, lakes, or coastal areas, learning about the factors that impact water quality and the importance of clean water.

Affordable and Clean Energy

Ensure access to affordable, reliable, sustainable, and modern energy for all.

Aims to increase the share of renewable energy in the global energy mix, improve energy efficiency, and enhance the infrastructure and technology for supplying modern and sustainable energy services in all countries, particularly in developing regions.

This includes expanding infrastructure and upgrading technology to provide clean energy sources in developing countries.

- Solar Science Projects: Introduce students to renewable energy by installing solar panels on campus and using them as practical tools for science classes to learn about clean energy production.
- Energy Audit Programs: Students can participate in or lead energy audits for their school or college to understand energy consumption patterns and propose ways to reduce energy use and transition to renewable sources.

Climate Action

Take urgent action to combat climate change and its impacts.

Underscores the need to strengthen resilience and adaptive capacity to climate-related hazards and natural disasters. It involves integrating climate change measures into national policies and strategies, improving education and awareness on climate change mitigation, adaptation, and impact reduction. It also calls for enhanced institutional capacity on climate change-related planning and management.

- Climate Change Education Modules: Incorporate comprehensive climate change education into the science curriculum to cover topics such as global warming, greenhouse gases, and the impact of human activities on climate.
- Eco-friendly Initiatives: Promote initiatives like carpooling, biking to school, or using public transportation to reduce the carbon footprint associated with commuting.

Life below Water

Conserve and sustainably use the oceans, seas, and marine resources for sustainable development.

Focuses on conserving marine and coastal ecosystems to avoid significant adverse impacts, managing and protecting marine and coastal ecosystems to achieve healthy and productive oceans. It includes preventing and reducing marine pollution of all kinds, particularly from land-based activities, including marine debris and nutrient pollution.

- Marine Biology Field Trips: Organize field trips to coastal and marine environments where students can learn about marine ecosystems, the importance of biodiversity, and human impacts on these habitats.
- Beach Clean-Up Days: Schools and colleges can organize regular clean-up events at nearby beaches to raise awareness about marine pollution, particularly plastic waste, and its effects on marine life.

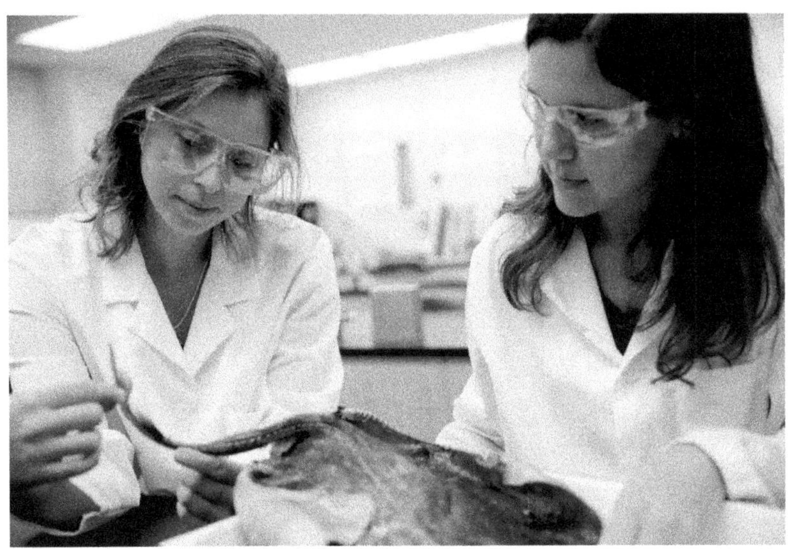

Life on Land

Protect, restore, and promote sustainable use of terrestrial ecosystems, sustainably manage forests, combat desertification, and halt and reverse land degradation and biodiversity loss.

Aims to ensure the conservation, restoration, and sustainable use of terrestrial and inland freshwater ecosystems and their services. It calls for urgent action to end deforestation, and substantially increase afforestation and reforestation globally. It also focuses on conserving mountain ecosystems, including their biodiversity, to enhance their capacity to provide benefits essential for sustainable development.

- Reforestation Projects: Students can participate in or initiate tree planting days to help reforest local areas, learn about the role of trees in maintaining ecological balance, and combat land degradation.
- Wildlife Conservation Clubs: Establish clubs or societies focused on wildlife conservation that can spearhead

awareness campaigns, support local wildlife reserves, and educate peers about endangered species and habitat preservation.

Prosperity

Prosperity Pillar is about fostering economic growth in a way that ensures all individuals benefit from it without compromising the environment. It involves creating opportunities for people to achieve their potential in a thriving economy that uses resources wisely and minimizes waste and pollution.

No Poverty

End poverty in all its forms everywhere.

Aims to eradicate extreme poverty (those living on less than $1.90 a day) and reduce the proportion of men, women, and children of all ages living in poverty in all its dimensions according to national definitions. It involves measures to ensure that the poor and vulnerable have equal rights to economic resources, access to basic services, ownership, and control over land and other forms of property, inheritance, natural resources, appropriate new technology, and financial services.

- Community Engagement Projects: Schools and colleges can develop programs where students volunteer or work on projects aimed at alleviating poverty in local communities. For example, setting up food banks, offering tutoring services to underprivileged children, or assisting in shelters.
- Entrepreneurship Training: Provide students with the skills to start their own businesses, with a focus on social entrepreneurship that aims to solve community problems such as poverty.

Decent Work and Economic Growth

Promote sustained, inclusive, and sustainable economic growth, full and productive employment, and decent work for all.

Focuses on achieving higher levels of economic productivity through diversification, technological upgrading, and innovation. It emphasizes the need for decent job creation, entrepreneurship, creativity, and innovation, and encourages the formalization and growth of micro, small, and medium-sized enterprises including through access to financial services.

- Career and Technical Education (CTE) Programs: Offer programs that equip students with specific vocational skills that are in demand in the local economy, thus improving their employability upon graduation.
- Internship Programs: Develop partnerships with local businesses to provide students with internship opportunities, giving them real-world experience and potentially improving job prospects.

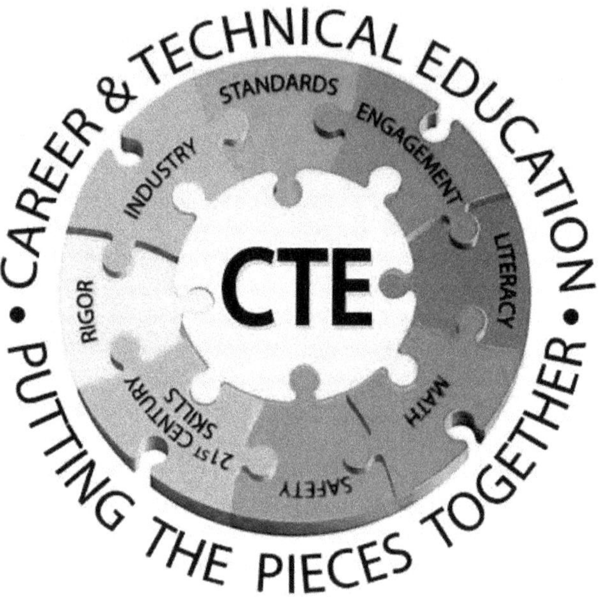

Industry, Innovation, and Infrastructure

Build resilient infrastructure, promote inclusive and sustainable industrialization, and foster innovation.

Advocates for building robust infrastructure to support economic development and human well-being, with a focus on equitable access for all. It aims to promote inclusive and sustainable industrialization, and by 2030 significantly raise industry's share of employment and GDP. The goal is to enhance scientific research, upgrade the technological capabilities of industrial sectors in all countries, and encourage innovation.

- Innovation Labs: Establish innovation labs on campus where students can use technology to create prototypes or develop new products, fostering a spirit of innovation and creativity.
- Support for Student Startups: Provide resources such as seed funding, mentoring, and office space to help student-led startups that focus on sustainable industries and technologies.

Reduced Inequalities

Objective: Reduce inequality within and among countries.

Seeks to ensure that income growth of the bottom 40% of the population is greater than the national average, which will help achieve greater equality. It also focuses on promoting the social, economic, and political inclusion of all, irrespective of age, sex, disability, race, ethnicity, origin, religion, or economic or other status. Additionally, it involves facilitating orderly, safe, and responsible migration and mobility of people, including through the implementation of planned and well-managed migration policies.

- Scholarship Programs: Develop scholarship programs aimed at students from disadvantaged backgrounds to ensure that higher education is accessible to all, regardless of economic status.
- Inclusive Education Policies: Implement policies that support the inclusion of all students, including those with disabilities, ensuring that everyone has equal access to educational opportunities.

Responsible Consumption and Production

Ensure sustainable consumption and production patterns aims to promote resource and energy efficiency, sustainable infrastructure, and providing access to basic services, green and decent jobs, and a better quality of life for all. It involves engaging businesses, creating awareness, and fostering a culture of sustainability in consumption and production. The goal highlights the need for a systemic approach and cooperation among actors operating in the supply chain, from producer to final consumer.

- Sustainability Workshops: Conduct workshops and seminars on sustainable consumption practices, teaching students how to minimize waste and make environmentally friendly choices.
- Recycling and Upcycling Projects: Encourage recycling initiatives on campus and support student projects that focus on upcycling materials that would otherwise be discarded.

People

People pillar centers on ensuring that all human beings can enjoy prosperous and fulfilling lives and that economic, social, and technological progress occurs in harmony with nature. It is focused on enhancing health, education, and social inclusion.

Zero Hunger

End hunger, achieve food security and improved nutrition, and promote sustainable agriculture.

Aims to ensure that everyone has access to sufficient and nutritious food all year round. This involves promoting sustainable agricultural practices, supporting small-scale farmers and equal access to land, technology, and markets. It also requires international cooperation to ensure investment in infrastructure and technology to improve agricultural productivity.

- Nutritional Programs: Implement school feeding programs that provide nutritious meals to students, ensuring they have the necessary energy and health to engage in learning.
- Educational Gardens: Create school gardens where students can learn about sustainable agriculture and the importance of nutrition, while producing fresh food for school meals or local communities.

Good Health and Well-being

Ensure healthy lives and promote well-being for all at all ages.

About ensuring that people can live healthy lives and that countries can help their populations achieve this. This goal includes a wide range of objectives, from reducing maternal and child mortality to fighting diseases such as AIDS, malaria, and other communicable diseases. It also aims to ensure universal health coverage and access to safe and effective medicines and vaccines for all.

- Health Education: Integrate comprehensive health education into the curriculum, covering topics from basic hygiene practices to more complex issues like mental health and wellness.

- Wellness Activities: Offer wellness programs that include physical activities, meditation sessions, and workshops on stress management to promote mental and physical health among students.

Quality Education

Ensure inclusive and equitable quality education and promote lifelong learning opportunities for all.

Regardless of age, everyone should have access to quality educational opportunities. This aims to significantly increase literacy and numeracy among youth and adults and ensure that all youth and a substantial proportion of adults achieve literacy and numeracy. The goal is to eliminate gender and wealth disparities and ensure equitable access to all levels of education and vocational training.

- Technology Integration: Enhance learning experiences by integrating technology in classrooms, providing students with access to digital learning tools and resources.

- Skill-Based Learning: Develop programs that focus on practical skills, critical thinking, and problem-solving, preparing students for real-world challenges.

Gender Equality

Achieve gender equality and empower all women and girls.

Ensures that women and girls achieve full equality in all aspects of life. This includes ending discrimination and violence against women and girls, ensuring women's full and

effective participation and equal opportunities for leadership at all levels of decision-making in political, economic, and public life. It also includes ensuring universal access to sexual and reproductive health and rights.

- Awareness Campaigns: Conduct campaigns and workshops to raise awareness about gender equality, discussing topics such as gender roles, rights, and empowerment.
- Support Groups: Establish support groups and mentorship programs that encourage female students to pursue careers in fields traditionally dominated by men, such as STEM.

Sustainable Cities and Communities

Focuses on making cities and human settlements inclusive, safe, resilient, and sustainable. It involves investing in public transport, creating green public spaces, and improving urban planning and management in participatory and inclusive ways. This goal also aims to reduce the adverse per capita environmental impact of cities, including paying special attention to air quality and municipal and other waste management.

- Urban Planning Projects: Engage students in projects that simulate urban planning and sustainable community development, encouraging them to think about how cities can be designed to be more livable and sustainable.
- Community Service Initiatives: Facilitate community service opportunities that allow students to contribute to improving their local environments, such as participating in local clean-up days or helping to build community centers.

Peace, Justice, and Strong Institutions

Promote peaceful and inclusive societies for sustainable development, provide access to justice for all, and build effective, accountable, and inclusive institutions at all levels.

Involves reducing all forms of violence, working with governments and communities to find lasting solutions to conflict and insecurity. Strengthening the rule of law and promoting human rights is key to this process, as is reducing the flow of illicit arms and strengthening the participation of developing countries in the institutions of global governance.

- Civic Education: Provide civic education that teaches students about their rights, the importance of the rule of law, and how to engage with institutions responsibly and effectively.
- Conflict Resolution Workshops: Offer workshops on conflict resolution and peacebuilding, equipping students

with the skills to manage and resolve disputes peacefully and constructively.

Partnerships

Recognizing that sustainable development goals cannot be achieved by any one entity alone, this pillar emphasizes the importance of partnerships between governments, the private sector, and civil society. These relationships facilitate knowledge sharing, technical and logistic support, and collaborative solutions to complex challenges.

Global collaboration:

Promote global collaboration among countries and emphasis on international partnerships.

It aims to collaborate and join hands with world class countries to encourage global partnerships and call for action by all the countries and ensure no one is left behind.

Partnerships for the Goals

Strengthen the means of implementation and revitalize the global partnership for sustainable development.

About enhancing global partnerships that mobilize and share knowledge, expertise, technology, and financial resources to support the achievement of the sustainable development goals in all countries. It emphasizes the role of partnerships between governments, the private sector, and civil society to achieve sustainable development.

Chapter 6:

The Importance of Sustainability in Today's World:

Sustainability encompasses environmental, social, and economic dimensions, all of which are interconnected and essential for human flourishing. In today's world, the importance of sustainability cannot be overstated for several reasons:

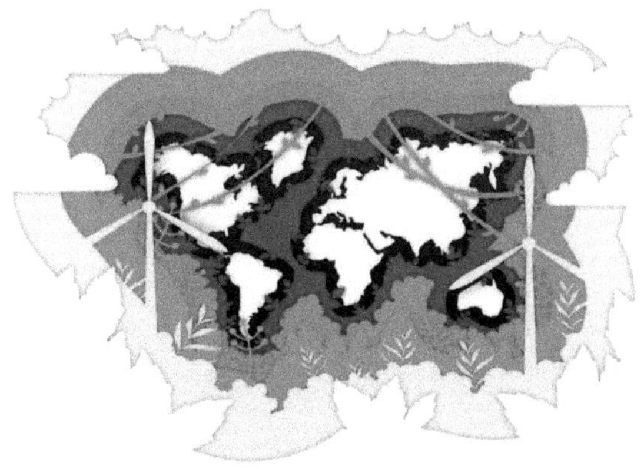

1. Environmental Preservation: With ecosystems under strain from pollution, deforestation, and habitat destruction, adopting sustainable practices is critical for safeguarding biodiversity and protecting vital natural resources.
2. Climate Change Mitigation: Humanity faces the existential threat of climate change, driven primarily by greenhouse gas emissions. Transitioning to renewable energy sources, reducing carbon footprints, and implementing sustainable land-use practices are imperative to mitigate climate change's adverse effects.

3. Social Equity and Justice: Sustainable development promotes social equity by ensuring that all individuals have access to basic needs such as clean water, nutritious food, and adequate shelter. Addressing issues of poverty, inequality, and social injustice is integral to achieving sustainable societies.
4. Economic Resilience: promotes innovation, resource efficiency, and long-term stability. Businesses that prioritize sustainability are better positioned to adapt to changing market dynamics and emerging environmental regulations.

Gaps in Sustainability Mindset of People:

Despite increasing awareness of sustainability issues, notable gaps in the mindset necessary to drive meaningful change:

1. Short-term Thinking: Many individuals and organizations prioritize short-term gains over long-term sustainability. This mindset often leads to unsustainable practices that compromise future well-being for immediate profits or convenience.

2. Lack of Systems Thinking: Sustainability requires a holistic understanding of complex systems and their interconnections. However, many decision-makers operate within narrow silos, overlooking the broader implications of their actions on the environment and society.
3. Disconnect from Nature: In an increasingly urbanized world, there is a growing disconnect between people and the natural world. This disconnection can diminish appreciation for the environment and hinder efforts to promote sustainable behaviors.
4. Resistance to Change: Embracing sustainability often necessitates changes in behavior, consumption patterns, and economic systems. Resistance to change, whether due to inertia, vested interests, or fear of the unknown, poses a significant barrier to progress.

Addressing the Gaps:

To bridge the gaps in the sustainability mindset and enable meaningful action, concerted efforts are needed at individual, institutional, and societal levels:

1. Education and Awareness: Increasing public awareness and providing education on sustainability issues are essential for fostering a culture of sustainability. Empowering individuals with knowledge equips them to make informed choices and advocate for change.
2. Policy and Regulation: Governments play a crucial role in shaping the regulatory framework and incentivizing sustainable practices. Implementing policies that internalize environmental and social costs can drive market transformation toward sustainability.
3. Collaboration and Partnership: Addressing sustainability challenges requires collaboration across sectors and stakeholders. Partnerships between governments,

businesses, civil society organizations, and communities can catalyze collective action and innovation.

4. Empowering Future Generations: Investing in youth empowerment and leadership development is vital for building a sustainable future. Engaging young people in sustainability initiatives fosters a sense of ownership and responsibility for shaping a more equitable and resilient world.

Sustainability is paramount in today's world to address pressing environmental, social, and economic challenges. However, realizing a sustainable future requires closing the gaps in the sustainability mindset and embracing a holistic approach to decision-making and action. By fostering a culture of sustainability, empowering individuals, and fostering collaboration, we can pave the way for a more equitable, resilient, and flourishing planet for generations to come.

How does each pillar contribute to sustainability?

The ZHA Sustainability Mindset Framework focuses on four pillars: Planet, People, Partnership, and Prosperity. Each of these pillars contributes to sustainability by addressing specific aspects of environmental, social, and economic well-being. Here's how each pillar contributes to sustainability:

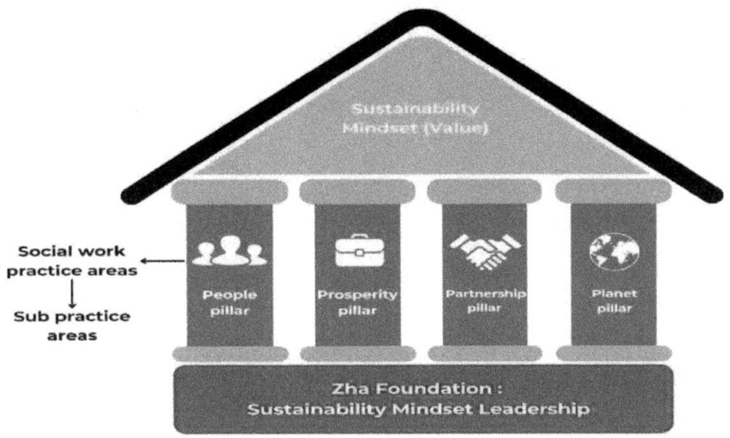

1. Planet

Contribution to Sustainability:

- **Environmental Stewardship**: The Planet pillar emphasizes the importance of protecting and restoring natural ecosystems. This includes practices such as conservation, reforestation, and sustainable resource management, which help maintain biodiversity and ecological balance.
- **Climate Action**: It promotes actions to mitigate climate change, such as reducing greenhouse gas emissions, adopting renewable energy sources, and enhancing energy efficiency. These actions are crucial for stabilizing the climate and reducing the impacts of global warming.
- **Sustainable Practices**: Encourages the adoption of sustainable agricultural, industrial, and consumption

practices that minimize environmental degradation and reduce the ecological footprint of human activities.

2. People

Contribution to Sustainability:

- **Social Equity**: The People pillar focuses on promoting social justice and equity. It ensures that all individuals, regardless of their background, have access to basic needs such as clean water, nutritious food, education, healthcare, and safe living conditions.
- **Community Well-Being**: It fosters strong, healthy, and resilient communities by promoting inclusive and participatory decision-making processes. This includes engaging communities in sustainability initiatives and ensuring their voices are heard.
- **Human Rights**: Advocates for the protection of human rights and dignity, addressing issues such as labor rights, gender equality, and the rights of indigenous peoples. This creates a fairer and more just society.

3. Partnership

Contribution to Sustainability:

- **Collaboration**: The Partnership pillar underscores the importance of collaboration among various stakeholders, including governments, businesses, non-profits, and communities. By working together, these entities can pool resources, knowledge, and expertise to achieve common sustainability goals.

- **Public-Private Partnerships**: Encourages partnerships between the public and private sectors to drive innovation and investment in sustainable technologies and practices. This can lead to the development of scalable solutions to environmental and social challenges.

- **Global Cooperation**: Promotes international cooperation to address global sustainability issues such as climate change, biodiversity loss, and social inequalities. Collaborative efforts can lead to more effective and widespread solutions.

4. Prosperity

Contribution to Sustainability:

- **Economic Resilience**: The Prosperity pillar emphasizes the creation of resilient and inclusive economies that support sustainable development. This includes promoting sustainable business practices, fair trade, and economic diversification.

- **Inclusive Growth**: Advocates for economic growth that benefits all segments of society, particularly the marginalized and vulnerable. This ensures that economic development contributes to reducing poverty and inequality.

- **Innovation and Technology**: Encourages the development and adoption of sustainable technologies and innovative solutions that enhance efficiency, reduce waste, and create new opportunities for economic growth. This can drive progress towards a more sustainable and prosperous future.

Thus, Each pillar of the ZHA Sustainability Mindset Framework—Planet, People, Partnership, and Prosperity—plays a crucial role in promoting sustainability by addressing different aspects of environmental, social, and economic well-being.

- The **Planet** pillar ensures the protection and restoration of natural ecosystems and promotes climate action and sustainable practices.

- The **People** pillar focuses on social equity, community well-being, and human rights, fostering inclusive and fair societies.

- The **Partnership** pillar highlights the importance of collaboration and cooperation among various stakeholders to achieve shared sustainability goals.

- The **Prosperity** pillar aims to create resilient and inclusive economies that support sustainable development, inclusive growth, and technological innovation.

Together, these pillars create a comprehensive framework that equips individuals and organizations with the knowledge, values, and strategies needed to achieve a sustainable future.

Chapter 7:

The role of individuals in promoting sustainability clubs

In envisioning a sustainable future, individuals, often referred to as the common man or people, play a pivotal role. While large-scale initiatives and policies are essential, it is the collective actions of individuals that truly drive progress toward sustainability. This explores the role of individuals in promoting sustainability and highlights how their efforts contribute to building a more sustainable and prosperous world.

Empowering Individuals for Sustainability:

Conscious Consumption:

1. Individuals have the power to influence sustainability through their consumption choices. By opting for products and services that are ethically sourced, environmentally friendly, and socially responsible, individuals can drive demand for sustainable goods and services. This consumer behavior incentivizes businesses to adopt sustainable practices throughout their supply chains.

Sustainable Lifestyles:

2. Adopting sustainable lifestyles is another way individuals can contribute to sustainability. This includes practices such as reducing energy and water consumption, minimizing waste generation, practicing eco-friendly transportation methods, and embracing plant-based diets. By making conscious choices in their daily lives, individuals can reduce their ecological footprint and inspire others to do the same.

Advocacy and Education:

3. Individuals can also promote sustainability by raising awareness and advocating for change within their communities and beyond. Whether through social media activism, grassroots organizing, or participation in environmental campaigns, individuals have the power to amplify their voices and influence public opinion. Additionally, educating oneself and others about sustainability issues, solutions, and best practices is key to fostering a culture of sustainability.

Civic Engagement:

4. Engaging in civic activities, such as voting, petitioning policymakers, and participating in local governance, empowers individuals to shape sustainability policies and practices at the institutional level. By holding elected officials and decision-makers accountable for their actions, individuals can contribute to the development and implementation of policies that prioritize sustainability and environmental protection.

Adding Value to the Sustainable Future:

Environmental Preservation:

1. The collective actions of individuals in promoting sustainability contribute to environmental preservation and conservation efforts. By reducing resource consumption, minimizing pollution, and protecting natural habitats, individuals help safeguard biodiversity and mitigate the impacts of climate change.

Social Equity and Justice:

2. Sustainability is inherently linked to social equity and justice, as it seeks to ensure the well-being of all people, regardless of their socioeconomic status or background. By advocating for inclusive and equitable policies and practices, individuals can address systemic inequalities and promote social cohesion and solidarity within communities.

Economic Resilience and Innovation:

3. Embracing sustainability fosters economic resilience and innovation by encouraging resource efficiency, promoting green technologies, and creating new opportunities for green jobs and industries. By supporting sustainable businesses and entrepreneurship, individuals contribute to building a more robust and diversified economy that can thrive in a changing world.

4. Individuals play a crucial role in promoting sustainability and building a sustainable future. Through conscious consumption, sustainable lifestyles, advocacy, education, and civic engagement, individuals can contribute to environmental preservation, social equity, economic resilience, and innovation. By harnessing the collective power of people, we can create a world where sustainability is not just a goal but a way of life, enriching the lives of present and future generations.

5. Armed with insights from their observations and experiences, the Zha Foundation came to appreciate the importance of embedding sustainability principles into all aspects of human endeavor. This includes principles such as environmental stewardship, social equity, economic resilience, intergenerational justice, and systems thinking. Embracing these principles not only helps in addressing immediate challenges but also lays the foundation for a more sustainable and resilient future.

The Zha Foundation's journey toward understanding the importance of a sustainability mindset involved a process of observation, reflection, learning, and action over the past decade. By recognizing the interconnectedness of environmental, social, and economic issues and the consequences of unsustainable behavior, the foundation has been inspired to champion sustainability principles and work towards creating a more sustainable future for all.

Chapter 8:
Understanding Sustainability

Definition and Dimensions of Sustainability

Sustainability is a concept that encompasses a broad range of interrelated ideas and principles aimed at ensuring the long-term well-being of both present and future generations. At its core, sustainability seeks to balance economic, social, and environmental considerations.

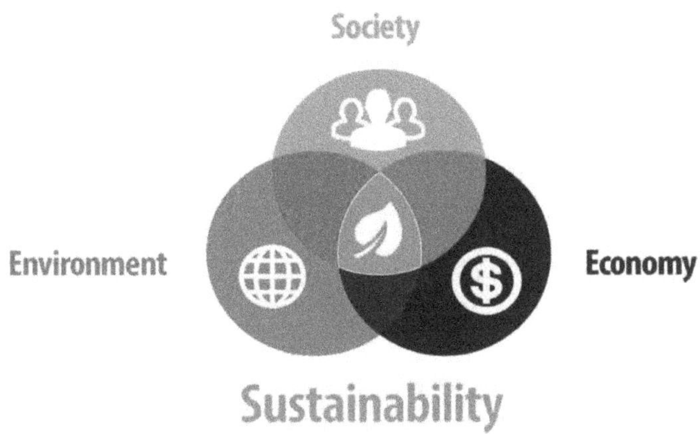

Let's explore the definition and dimensions of sustainability in more detail:

Definition of Sustainability:

Sustainability can be defined as the capacity to endure or persist over time while maintaining or improving the quality of life for current and future generations. It involves responsibly managing resources, minimizing environmental impacts, promoting social equity, and fostering economic prosperity in a way that does not deplete or degrade natural systems or compromise the ability of future generations to thrive.

Dimensions of Sustainability:

Sustainability is often described in terms of three interconnected dimensions, known as the triple bottom line or the three pillars of sustainability:

1. Environmental Dimension:

   The environmental dimension of sustainability focuses on protecting and preserving natural ecosystems, biodiversity, and resources. It involves practices aimed at minimizing pollution, reducing waste, conserving energy and water, promoting renewable energy sources, and mitigating and adapting to climate change. Environmental sustainability recognizes the intrinsic value of nature and seeks to maintain ecological balance for the benefit of all life forms on earth.

2. Social Dimension:

   The social dimension of sustainability pertains to ensuring social equity, justice, and well-being for all people, both within present and future generations. It involves addressing issues such as poverty, inequality, access to education and healthcare, human rights, social cohesion, and cultural diversity. Social sustainability emphasizes the importance of inclusive decision-making processes, equitable distribution of resources, and respect for human dignity and diversity.

3. Economic Dimension:

   The economic dimension of sustainability focuses on fostering economic prosperity and resilience while promoting responsible resource management and equitable distribution of wealth. It involves creating economic systems that are environmentally sound, socially just, and economically viable in the long term.

Economic sustainability encompasses principles of resource efficiency, innovation, ethical business practices, fair trade, and investment in sustainable infrastructure and technologies.

These three dimensions of sustainability are interconnected and mutually reinforcing, and they must be addressed in tandem to achieve holistic and enduring solutions to global challenges. Ignoring any one dimension can lead to imbalances that undermine the overall goal of sustainability. Therefore, sustainable development requires a comprehensive and integrated approach that considers the complex interactions between environmental, social, and economic systems.

Aligning ZHA Sustainability Mindset Methodology with UNESCO's 17 Sustainable Development Goals (SDGs)

The United Nations Educational, Scientific and Cultural Organization (UNESCO) contributes to the global effort to achieve sustainable development through its support and promotion of the 17 Sustainable Development Goals (SDGs). These goals were established by the United Nations in 2015 as part of the 2030 Agenda for Sustainable Development, which serves as a blueprint for addressing global challenges and improving the lives of people around the world. Let's explore each of the 17 SDGs and how UNESCO contributes to their achievement:

No Poverty:

1. It works to promote inclusive and equitable access to education, culture, and information as a means to eradicate poverty and reduce inequalities.

Zero Hunger:

2. Supports initiatives that enhance agricultural productivity, promote sustainable food systems, and improve access to education and information on nutrition and food security.

Good Health and Well-being:

3. Promotes health education, scientific research, and cultural activities that contribute to improving health outcomes and well-being for all.

Quality Education:

4. It focuses on ensuring inclusive and equitable quality education for all, promoting lifelong learning opportunities, and fostering educational innovation and excellence.

Gender Equality:

5. Advocates for gender equality in education, science, and culture, working to eliminate gender disparities and empower women and girls.

Clean Water and Sanitation:

6. Supports initiatives to improve water management, promote water education, and enhance access to safe drinking water and sanitation services.

Affordable and Clean Energy:

7. Promotes renewable energy technologies, energy efficiency, and sustainable energy policies to ensure access to affordable and clean energy for all.

Decent Work and Economic Growth:

8. It contributes to sustainable economic development by promoting skills development, entrepreneurship, and cultural industries that create decent jobs and foster inclusive growth.

Industry, Innovation, and Infrastructure:

9. Supports research, innovation, and technology transfer initiatives that drive sustainable industrialization and enhance infrastructure development

Reduced Inequality:.

10. It works to reduce inequalities within and among countries by promoting inclusive education, cultural diversity, and equal access to information and knowledge resources.

Sustainable Cities and Communities:

11. Supports efforts to promote sustainable urbanization, heritage conservation, and cultural diversity in cities and communities worldwide.

Responsible Consumption and Production:

12. Advocates for sustainable consumption and production patterns, promoting education, awareness, and capacity-building on resource efficiency and environmental sustainability.

Climate Action:

13. It addresses climate change through education, research, and policy support, promoting climate literacy, adaptation measures, and sustainable practices in various sectors.

Life Below Water:

14. Supports marine conservation efforts, promotes sustainable fisheries management, and fosters ocean literacy to protect and restore marine ecosystems.

Life on Land:

15. It works to conserve terrestrial ecosystems, promote biodiversity conservation, and combat desertification and land degradation through education and awareness-raising activities.

Peace, Justice, and Strong Institutions:

16. Promotes education for peace, human rights education, cultural heritage protection, and media freedom as pillars of sustainable development and peacebuilding.

Partnerships for the Goals:

17. It fosters global partnerships and collaboration to support the implementation of the SDGs, leveraging its networks, expertise, and resources to drive collective action for sustainable development.

Through its diverse programs and initiatives spanning education, science, culture, communication, and information, UNESCO plays a vital role in advancing the 2030 Agenda and contributing to the achievement of the Sustainable Development Goals.

Chapter 9:

Circular Economy is derived from Sustainability Mindset of People

The concept of a circular economy is an economic system designed to maximize the use of resources and minimize waste by keeping products, materials, and resources in use for as long as possible. Unlike the traditional linear economy, which follows a 'take-make-dispose' model, the circular economy aims to create a closed-loop system where resources are continuously recycled, reused, and regenerated to create new value.

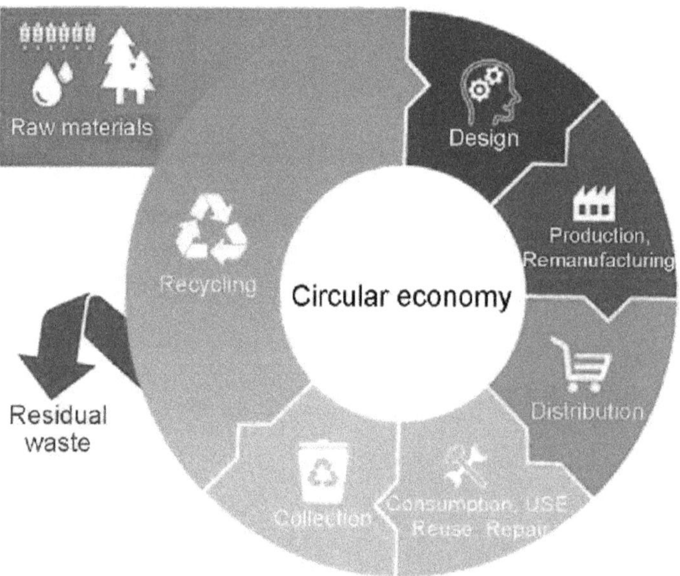

Key principles of a circular economy include:

1. Designing out Waste and Pollution: Products and systems are designed with the goal of eliminating waste and pollution at every stage of their lifecycle. This involves considering factors such as material selection, product durability, reparability, and recyclability from the outset.
2. Keeping Products and Materials in Use: Instead of discarding products after use, the circular economy seeks to extend their lifespan through practices such as repair, refurbishment, remanufacturing, and reuse. This prolongs the utility of products and reduces the need for new resource extraction.
3. Regenerating Natural Systems: The circular economy aims to restore and regenerate natural ecosystems by minimizing environmental impacts, conserving resources, and promoting regenerative practices such as sustainable agriculture, reforestation, and ecosystem restoration.
4. Closing the Loop of Material Flows: Resources are recovered and recycled at the end of their life to create new products, materials, and resources. This involves implementing efficient recycling infrastructure, developing innovative technologies for resource recovery, and fostering circular supply chains.
5. Collaboration and Innovation: Collaboration among stakeholders, including businesses, governments, academia, and civil society, is essential for driving innovation and scaling up circular solutions. This includes sharing knowledge, executing best practices, and resources to overcome barriers and accelerate the transition to a circular economy.

Benefits of a circular economy include:

- Resource Efficiency: By maximizing the use of existing resources and minimizing waste, a circular economy reduces resource extraction, energy consumption, and environmental degradation, leading to greater resource efficiency and resilience.
- Economic Opportunities: The circular economy presents economic opportunities through job creation, innovation, and the development of new markets for recycled materials, products, and services. It also reduces business risks associated with resource scarcity and price volatility.
- Environmental Sustainability: By promoting sustainable consumption and production patterns, the circular economy contributes to environmental sustainability by reducing greenhouse gas emissions, pollution, and habitat destruction.
- Social Inclusivity: A circular economy can contribute to social inclusivity by creating jobs, fostering local economies, and promoting access to affordable, durable, and environmentally friendly products and services.

Overall, the concept of a circular economy offers a promising framework for achieving sustainable development by decoupling economic growth from resource consumption and environmental degradation. It represents a fundamental shift in how we produce, consume, and value goods and services, with the potential to create a more resilient, equitable, and prosperous future for all.

ZSPC Inner Vision for Creating Circular Economy Practices through our Social Work Practices

Our vision at ZSPC is to foster and implement circular economy practices through dedicated social work initiatives. We aim to integrate these principles into our social work practices, ensuring that every action contributes to a sustainable, regenerative system that benefits both society and the environment.

Key Components of the Vision

1. **Education and Awareness**
   - **Community Education**: Educate communities about the benefits of a circular economy, including reduced waste, resource conservation, and economic opportunities.
   - **School Programs**: Integrate circular economy principles into school curricula to instill sustainable habits and mindsets from a young age.
2. **Resource Management**
   - **Recycling and Upcycling Initiatives**: Develop programs that promote the recycling and upcycling of materials to reduce waste and extend the lifecycle of products.
   - **Waste Reduction Campaigns**: Implement campaigns that encourage waste reduction practices, such as composting, minimal packaging, and mindful consumption.

3. **Sustainable Consumption**

    - **Community Workshops**: Conduct workshops that teach sustainable consumption practices, such as buying second-hand, repairing instead of replacing, and choosing eco-friendly products.

    - **Local Business Support**: Partner with local businesses to promote and adopt circular practices, such as using recycled materials and offering repair services.

4. **Economic Opportunities**

    - **Job Creation**: Create job opportunities in the recycling, repair, and upcycling sectors, contributing to economic resilience and social inclusion.

    - **Entrepreneurship Support**: Support entrepreneurship in the circular economy by providing training, resources, and mentorship for start-ups focused on sustainable solutions.

5. **Collaboration and Partnerships**

    - **Public-Private Partnerships**: Foster partnerships between public entities, private companies, and non-profits to drive collective action towards circular economy goals.

    - **Global Networks**: Engage with global networks to share best practices, innovations, and resources for circular economy implementation.

6. **Policy Advocacy**

   - **Regulatory Support**: Advocate for policies that support circular economy practices, such as extended producer responsibility, waste reduction targets, and incentives for sustainable businesses.

   - **Community Engagement**: Involve communities in policy-making processes to ensure that local needs and perspectives are reflected in sustainability initiatives.

Implementation Strategy

1. **Assessment and Planning**

   - **Community Needs Assessment**: Conduct assessments to understand the specific needs and opportunities for circular economy practices within communities.

   - **Strategic Planning**: Develop strategic plans that outline clear goals, actions, and timelines for implementing circular economy practices.

2. **Capacity Building**

   - **Training Programs**: Offer training programs for social workers, educators, and community leaders to equip them with the knowledge and skills to promote circular economy practices.

   - **Resource Development**: Create and distribute educational materials, toolkits, and resources to support the adoption of circular practices.

3. **Monitoring and Evaluation**

    - **Impact Assessment**: Regularly assess the impact of circular economy initiatives to measure progress, identify challenges, and make data-driven adjustments.

    - **Feedback Mechanisms**: Establish feedback mechanisms to gather input from community members and stakeholders, ensuring continuous improvement and relevance.

Thus, Our vision at ZSPC is to create and sustain circular economy practices through comprehensive social work initiatives. By focusing on education, resource management, sustainable consumption, economic opportunities, collaboration, and policy advocacy, we aim to build a resilient and sustainable society. Through these efforts, we strive to create a regenerative system that not only reduces waste and conserves resources but also fosters social and economic well-being for all.

Chapter 10:

Role of ZHA Sustainability Social Coaches for Implementing the Curriculum

The ZHA Foundation aims to create the role of Sustainability Social Coaches to facilitate the implementation of the curriculum developed for the Zha Sustainability Practitioners Club. These coaches will serve as mentors, educators, and facilitators, guiding club members through the learning process and helping them apply sustainability principles in their personal and professional lives.

Here are the steps to implement the curriculum focusing on the ZHA Sustainability for People Framework:

Curriculum Design:

1. The ZHA Foundation collaborates with subject matter experts, educators, and sustainability practitioners to design a comprehensive curriculum based on the ZHA Sustainability for People Framework. The curriculum covers key topics, learning objectives, activities, and

resources aligned with the framework's pillars and principles.

Recruitment and Training of Sustainability Social Coaches:

2. The foundation recruits qualified individuals with expertise in sustainability, education, coaching, and community engagement to serve as Sustainability Social Coaches. Coaches undergo training on the curriculum, coaching techniques, facilitation skills, and effective communication strategies to support club members in their sustainability journey.

Curriculum Implementation Plan:

3. The foundation develops a detailed implementation plan outlining the schedule, structure, and delivery methods for the curriculum. The plan includes timelines, milestones, and evaluation criteria to ensure the curriculum's effective rollout and impact assessment.

Launch and Promotion:

4. The ZHA Foundation launches the Zha Sustainability Practitioners Club and promotes membership opportunities to individuals interested in learning and promoting sustainability practices. The club's mission, vision, goals, and benefits are communicated through various channels, including social media, newsletters, and outreach events.

Orientation and Onboarding:

5. Club members undergo an orientation session to familiarize themselves with the club's objectives, expectations, and activities. They receive access to the curriculum, resources, and support materials, as well as guidance on how to engage with Sustainability Social Coaches and fellow club members.

Curriculum Delivery:

6. Sustainability Social Coaches facilitate the delivery of the curriculum through a combination of in-person meetings, virtual sessions, workshops, and online platforms. They guide club members through interactive discussions, experiential learning activities, case studies, and practical exercises to deepen their understanding of sustainability concepts and practices.

Ongoing Support and Mentoring:

7. Sustainability Social Coaches provide ongoing support, mentoring, and feedback to club members throughout their learning journey. They offer guidance, encouragement, and resources to help members overcome challenges, set goals, and implement sustainability initiatives in their personal and professional lives.

Evaluation and Continuous Improvement:

8. The ZHA Foundation regularly evaluates the effectiveness of the curriculum and coaching process through feedback surveys, assessments, and performance indicators. Based on the feedback received, the foundation makes adjustments, updates, to the curriculum to ensure its relevance, engagement, and impact.

By implementing these steps, the ZHA Foundation can effectively deliver the curriculum focusing on the ZHA Sustainability for People Framework through the Zha Sustainability Practitioners Club, with Sustainability Social Coaches playing a crucial role in guiding and empowering club members to embrace sustainability principles and practices in their daily lives.

Chapter 11:

The human-centered approach to sustainability education

A human-centered approach to sustainability education is essential to the ZSPC because it prioritizes the needs, values, and behaviors of individuals and communities. By making sustainability education relevant, inclusive, and practical, this approach fosters engagement, promotes equity, encourages innovation, and builds strong, resilient communities. Ultimately, it ensures that sustainability principles are deeply embedded in the social fabric, driving lasting positive change for the environment and society.

Also ZHA Sustainability Mindset Framework, which integrates pillars such as Planet, People, Prosperity, and Partnership focuses on Human Centered Approach. A human-centered approach to sustainability education is fundamental to the ZHA Sustainability Process and Curriculum (ZSPC) because it places individuals and communities at the heart of sustainable development.

This approach recognizes that human behavior, values, and social systems are critical to achieving sustainability goals.

Here's how this approach is embedded in the framework:

Planet:

1. The Planet pillar acknowledges the interconnectedness between human well-being and environmental health. It emphasizes the importance of understanding and protecting the Earth's ecosystems, biodiversity, and natural resources to ensure a sustainable future for all. It involves raising awareness about environmental issues, promoting eco-conscious behaviors, and fostering a sense of stewardship and responsibility for the planet among individuals and communities.

People:

2. The People pillar focuses on promoting social equity, justice, and inclusivity as essential components of sustainability. It recognizes that sustainable development must prioritize the well-being and rights of all people, especially those who are marginalized or vulnerable. It involves empowering individuals with knowledge, skills, and opportunities to address social challenges, advocate for human rights, and promote diversity, equity, and inclusion in society.

Prosperity:

3. The Prosperity pillar highlights the importance of economic development that is inclusive, resilient, and environmentally sustainable.

   It emphasizes the need to create economic opportunities, reduce poverty, and ensure access to basic needs while safeguarding natural resources and ecosystems. It involves promoting responsible consumption and production patterns, fostering entrepreneurship and innovation, and equipping individuals with the skills and resources to build sustainable livelihoods and resilient communities.

Partnership:

4. The Partnership pillar emphasizes the value of collaboration, cooperation, and collective action in addressing global sustainability challenges. It recognizes that no single entity or sector can achieve sustainability alone and that partnerships among governments, businesses, civil society, and communities are essential for driving meaningful change.

   It involves fostering a spirit of collaboration, empathy, and solidarity among individuals and groups, promoting dialogue, building trust, and working together to find innovative solutions to complex problems.

By embedding a human-centered approach in the ZHA Sustainability Mindset

With pillars focusing on Planet, People, Prosperity, and Partnership, the framework recognizes the intrinsic connection between human well-being and environmental sustainability.

It underscores the importance of empowering individuals with the knowledge, values, and skills needed to address sustainability challenges, ultimately contributing to a more equitable, resilient, and prosperous future for all.

Benefits of Joining the Zha Foundation's ZSPC for Enabling the Sustainability Mindset for People:

Access to Educational Resources:

1. Members of the Zha Sustainability Practitioners Club gain access to educational resources, including the Zha Sustainability Mindset Framework, curricula, toolkits, case studies, and online courses, designed to enhance their understanding of sustainability principles and practices.

Professional Development Opportunities:

2. The club offers various professional development opportunities, such as workshops, seminars, webinars, and conferences, where members can learn from experts, gain new skills, and stay updated on emerging trends and best practices in sustainability.

Networking and Collaboration:

3. Membership in the club provides opportunities for networking and collaboration with like-minded individuals, organizations, and institutions committed to

advancing sustainability goals. Members can connect with peers, mentors, and potential partners to exchange ideas, share resources, and collaborate on projects that promote sustainability.

Mentorship and Guidance:

4. The club offers mentorship and guidance from experienced sustainability practitioners who can provide advice, support, and encouragement to members as they navigate their sustainability journey. Mentors offer insights, share lessons learned, and provide guidance on how to overcome challenges and achieve success in promoting sustainability.

Advocacy and Impact:

5. By joining the global movement led by the Zha Foundation, members can amplify their voices, advocate for policy changes, and drive collective action to align with government policies, international frameworks such as the United Nations Sustainable Development Goals (SDGs), and UNESCO goals. Through advocacy efforts and collaborative initiatives, members can make a meaningful impact on local, national, and global sustainability challenges.

In summary, the Zha Foundation's approach to implementing the Sustainability Mindset for People Initiative, including the development of the Zha Sustainability Mindset Framework and the establishment of the Zha Sustainability Practitioners Club, offers individuals opportunities to learn, collaborate, and contribute to the global sustainability movement. By joining this global movement, individuals can gain access to educational resources, professional development opportunities, networking and collaboration platforms, mentorship and guidance, and avenues for advocacy and impact, enabling them to align with government policies and UNESCO goals and promote a sustainability mindset for people worldwide

Chapter 12:

Key Components of the ZHA Methodology for Sustainability Mindset

The ZHA Methodology for Sustainability Mindset is designed to foster a comprehensive understanding and practice of sustainability principles among individuals and communities. This methodology integrates key components and social work practices that align people with the principles of a sustainability mindset through its framework.

1. Holistic Education

Sub-Practice Areas:

- **Interdisciplinary Learning**: Integrating subjects like science, economics, sociology, and ethics to provide a well-rounded understanding of sustainability.
- **Environmental Literacy**: Teaching the basics of ecology, climate science, and environmental stewardship.
- **Critical Thinking**: Developing analytical skills to assess sustainability issues and solutions.

Alignment with Sustainability Principles:

- Promotes a deep understanding of the interconnectedness of environmental, social, and economic systems.
- Encourages informed decision-making based on a comprehensive understanding of sustainability.

2. Active Engagement

Sub-Practice Areas:

- **Community Projects**: Involving students and community members in local sustainability initiatives such as clean-up drives, tree planting, and community gardens.
- **Service Learning**: Combining academic learning with community service to address real-world sustainability challenges.
- **Hands-On Activities**: Practical exercises that apply classroom knowledge to real-life situations, such as recycling programs and energy audits.

Alignment with Sustainability Principles:

- Enhances practical understanding and personal responsibility.
- Fosters a sense of community and collective action towards sustainability goals.

3. Critical Thinking and Innovation

Sub-Practice Areas:

- **Problem-Solving Workshops**: Sessions focused on identifying and addressing sustainability challenges through creative thinking.
- **Innovation Labs**: Spaces where students can experiment with sustainable technologies and practices.
- **Entrepreneurship Programs**: Encouraging the development of sustainable business ideas and startups.

Alignment with Sustainability Principles:

- Encourages innovation and the development of new, sustainable solutions.
- Promotes adaptability and resilience in the face of environmental and social changes.

4. Global and Local Perspectives

Sub-Practice Areas:

- **Global Awareness Programs**: Educating about global sustainability issues and the impact of local actions on the global stage.
- **Local Contextualization**: Adapting global sustainability principles to fit local cultural, economic, and environmental contexts.
- **Cross-Cultural Exchanges**: Programs that facilitate understanding and collaboration between different cultures and regions.

Alignment with Sustainability Principles:

- Balances global sustainability needs with local realities and practices.
- Fosters global citizenship and responsibility.

5. Ethical Responsibility

Sub-Practice Areas:

- **Ethics Courses**: Classes focused on the ethical dimensions of sustainability, including justice, equity, and stewardship.
- **Value-Based Education**: Integrating core values such as empathy, responsibility, and fairness into the curriculum.
- **Advocacy and Leadership Training**: Preparing students to be advocates for ethical and sustainable practices.

Alignment with Sustainability Principles:

- Instills a strong sense of ethical responsibility towards the environment and society.
- Encourages actions that are fair, just, and considerate of future generations.

Social Work Practices and Sub-Practice Areas of the Sustainability Mindset Framework

1. Awareness and Education Campaigns

Sub-Practice Areas:

- **Workshops and Seminars**: Conducting educational sessions on various aspects of sustainability.
- **Public Awareness Campaigns**: Utilizing media and community events to spread information about sustainability issues and solutions.

Alignment with Sustainability Principles:

- Raises awareness and educates the public on the importance of sustainable practices.
- Empowers individuals with the knowledge to make sustainable choices.

2. Community Development and Empowerment

Sub-Practice Areas:

- **Capacity Building**: Training community members in sustainable practices and leadership skills.
- **Resource Management Programs**: Helping communities develop sustainable ways to manage local resources such as water, soil, and energy.
- **Social Equity Initiatives**: Addressing social inequalities that impact sustainability, ensuring all community members benefit from sustainable development.

Alignment with Sustainability Principles:

- Builds resilient communities that can sustainably manage their resources.
- Promotes social equity and inclusivity.

3. Advocacy and Policy Influence

Sub-Practice Areas:

- **Policy Development**: Working with local governments to develop and implement policies that support sustainability.
- **Grassroots Advocacy**: Mobilizing community members to advocate for sustainable practices and policies.

- **Coalition Building**: Forming alliances with other organizations to strengthen advocacy efforts.

Alignment with Sustainability Principles:

- Influences policy to support sustainable development.
- Encourages community involvement in governance and policy-making.

4. Sustainable Economic Practices

Sub-Practice Areas:

- **Microfinance Programs**: Providing financial support for small-scale sustainable businesses.
- **Job Training**: Training individuals in skills needed for green jobs and sustainable industries.
- **Local Market Development**: Supporting the development of local markets for sustainable products.

Alignment with Sustainability Principles:

- Supports economic resilience through sustainable business practices.
- Encourages the development of a green economy that benefits the environment and society.

Implementation of Social Work Practices and Sub-Practice Areas

A methodology creates a path for you to follow, whereas a framework suggests what way to take a project such as curriculums for best practice learnings. The path is the Zha Sustainability Practitioners Club Model, and the way for us to adapt to sustainability mindset through the ZHA Sustainability Mindset

Framework, organized into pillars of **Planet, People, Prosperity, and Partnership**, serves as a comprehensive curriculum guide for fostering a sustainability mindset among students and people. Each pillar represents key components essential for understanding and embracing sustainability principles:

Planet:

Key Components:

- Environmental Conservation: Protecting and preserving natural ecosystems, biodiversity, and resources.
- Climate Action: Mitigating and adapting to climate change through sustainable practices and policies.
- Resource Management: Responsible stewardship of natural resources, including water, energy, and land.
- Connection with Sustainability Mindset: The Planet pillar emphasizes the interconnectedness between human activities and the health of the planet. Understanding the finite nature of resources and the impact of human actions on the environment is essential for developing a sustainability mindset.

People:

Key Components:

- Social Equity: Promoting fairness, justice, and inclusivity in society to ensure the well-being of all people.
- Human Rights: Upholding the rights and dignity of individuals, regardless of background or circumstances.
- Community Engagement: Empowering communities to participate in decision-making processes and advocate for their needs.
- Connection with Sustainability Mindset: The People pillar recognizes that sustainability is ultimately about improving the quality of life for all people. Fostering empathy, compassion, and a sense of social responsibility is crucial for developing a sustainability mindset that prioritizes the well-being of both present and future generations.

Prosperity:

Key Components:

- Economic Resilience: Building a diverse and sustainable economy that can withstand shocks and disruptions.
- Inclusive Growth: Creating economic opportunities and reducing poverty while minimizing inequalities.
- Sustainable Consumption: Promoting responsible consumption and production patterns that prioritize long-term well-being over short-term gains.
- Connection with Sustainability Mindset: The Prosperity pillar emphasizes the importance of balancing economic prosperity with social and environmental considerations. Recognizing the interdependence between economic, social, and environmental systems is essential for developing a sustainability mindset that prioritizes holistic well-being and resilience.

Partnership:

Key Components:

- Collaboration: Fostering partnerships and alliances among stakeholders to address shared sustainability challenges.
- Multisectoral Engagement: Involving governments, businesses, civil society, and communities in sustainability efforts.
- Knowledge Sharing: Sharing information, expertise, and best practices to drive collective action and innovation.
- Connection with Sustainability Mindset: The Partnership pillar underscores the importance of collaboration and cooperation in achieving sustainability goals. Recognizing the value of collective action and the power of partnerships is essential for developing a sustainability mindset that emphasizes collaboration, dialogue, and collective problem solving.

Implementation Plan for Mentoring Students and People Towards a Sustainable Mindset:

1. Curriculum Development:
   - Develop a comprehensive curriculum based on the Sustainability Mindset Framework, incorporating key components from each pillar.
   - Design educational materials, resources, and activities to engage students and people in learning about sustainability principles and practices.
2. Training and Capacity Building:
   - Train mentors, educators, and facilitators on the curriculum, coaching techniques, and sustainability principles.
   - Equip mentors with the skills and knowledge needed to guide students and people through the learning process and facilitate meaningful discussions and activities.

3. Outreach and Engagement:

    - Promote mentoring program and sustainability initiatives to students, educators, community members, and stakeholders.

    - Engage with schools, universities, community organizations, and businesses to recruit participants and foster partnerships.

4. Mentorship and Support:

    - Pair students and people with mentors who can provide guidance, support, and encouragement throughout their journey.

    - Offer ongoing mentorship, coaching sessions, and feedback to help individuals set goals, overcome challenges, and implement sustainability initiatives.

5. Experiential Learning:

    - Facilitate experiential learning opportunities, such as field trips, workshops, and service-learning projects, to deepen understanding and reinforce sustainability concepts.

    - Encourage hands-on activities, problem-solving exercises, and real-world applications to engage students and people in active learning and reflection.

6. Monitoring and Evaluation:

    - Regularly assess the effectiveness of the mentoring program and curriculum through feedback surveys, evaluations, and performance indicators.

- Gather data on participants' knowledge, attitudes, and behaviors related to sustainability to measure impact and identify areas for improvement.

7. Scaling Up and Sustainability:
    - Scale up the mentoring program and sustainability initiatives to reach a broader audience and expand impact.
    - Foster a culture of sustainability within schools, communities, and organizations by embedding sustainability principles into policies, practices, and decision-making processes.

Hence, By following this implementation plan, the Sustainability Mindset Framework can be effectively used for mentoring students and people towards a sustainable mindset.

Thus, the ZHA Methodology for Sustainability Mindset, with its key components and associated social work practices, effectively aligns individuals and communities with the principles of sustainability. By integrating holistic education, active engagement, critical thinking and innovation, global and local perspectives, and ethical responsibility, this methodology fosters a comprehensive and practical understanding of sustainability. Social work practices further reinforce these principles by raising awareness, empowering communities, influencing policy, and promoting sustainable economic practices. Together, these efforts create a strong foundation for sustainable development and a resilient future.

Chapter 13:

Twelve Sustainability Mindset Principles

"**Sustainability for People**" signifies a human-centered approach to sustainability, emphasizing the well-being and prosperity of current and future generations while respecting planetary boundaries. It goes beyond simply protecting the environment and considers the social, economic, and cultural dimensions of sustainability, ensuring that everyone has the opportunity to thrive within the limits of our planet.

The ZHA Foundation Charitable Trust envisions the establishment of the ZHA Sustainability Practitioners Club in various regions worldwide. This initiative aims to promote sustainability principles and values globally, fostering a mindset of environmental consciousness and social responsibility. The ZHA Sustainability Practitioners Club serves as a platform for individuals and organizations passionate about sustainability to connect, collaborate, and exchange ideas. Through various programs, workshops, and initiatives, the club aims to:

1. **Foster a Sustainability Mindset :** By promoting awareness and education on sustainability principles, the club encourages individuals to adopt environmentally conscious and socially responsible behaviors.

2. **Showcase Sustainable Practices :** Through case studies, best practices, and success stories, the club highlights innovative approaches to sustainability across different industries and sectors.

3. **Drive Collective Action :** By mobilizing resources and expertise, the club empowers members to initiate impactful projects and campaigns that contribute to sustainable development goals.

The ZHA Sustainability Practitioners follow the core 12 principles of a Sustainability Mindset,

The following Sustainability Mindset Principles are designed to guide individuals and organizations in adopting and promoting sustainable practices. These principles ensure a holistic approach to sustainability, integrating environmental, social, and economic dimensions.

1. **Feeling sufficient :** It could relate to concepts like lean thinking or sufficiency in resource consumption.
2. **Encouraging and Rewarding:** Rewarding and awarding the recognized people while they are alive and ensure everybody valuable persons in the society are recognized at the right moment
3. **Long-Term Thinking :** Emphasize decision-making that considers the long-term impacts on the environment, society, and economy, rather than focusing solely on short-term gains.
4. **Risk-based decision making :** It's part of a sustainability strategy, especially in terms of assessing and mitigating environmental and social risks.
5. **Gender equality :** To enable diverse perspectives, harmony and opportunities.
6. **Sharing and caring collaboration :** It emphasizes cooperation and collective action , creates more sustainable practitioners for environmental and social goals.
7. **Environmental Stewardship :** Take responsibility for protecting and preserving the natural environment, including biodiversity, ecosystems, and natural resources.

8. **Possessing a fail-fast approach helps in setting an appropriate vision :** Adopting a fail-fast approach is pivotal. It fosters an appreciation for adaptability, a core habit in sustainability, essential for crafting an appropriate vision.

9. **Community Engagement :** Involve stakeholders, including local communities, in decision-making processes to ensure that sustainability initiatives reflect their needs, concerns, and values.

10. **Social equality :** Strive for fairness and justice in addressing social issues such as poverty, inequality, and access to resources, ensuring that the benefits and burdens of sustainability efforts are distributed equitably.

11. **Continuous Learning and Improvement :** Embrace a culture of learning and reflection, continuously seeking opportunities to improve sustainability practices based on feedback, evaluation, and new information.

12. **Resource Conservation :** Prioritize the efficient use of natural resources, minimizing waste and promoting recycling and reuse wherever possible.

Case Study: Implementing Sustainability Mindset-Driven Principles through the ZHA Sustainability Practitioners Club

Background:

The ZHA Sustainability Practitioners Club (ZSPC) aimed to imbibe 12 Sustainability Driven Principles (SDPs) as part of its activities, with the goal of creating a mindset shift towards sustainable living and practices.

Implementation:

1. Principle Development: The ZHA Foundation collaborated with sustainability experts, thought leaders, and community members to identify and develop 12 Sustainability Driven Principles aligned with global sustainability goals and local context. These principles encompassed various aspects of sustainability, including environmental conservation, social equity, economic prosperity, and ethical governance.

2. Principle Integration: The 12 Sustainability Driven Principles were integrated into the club's activities, events, and initiatives to promote awareness, understanding, and adoption among members. Each principle was highlighted through themed workshops, discussions, case studies, and practical exercises.

3. Membership Engagement: Club members actively participated in discussions, debates, and activities centered around the 12 Sustainability Driven Principles. They shared insights, experiences, and best practices related to sustainability in their respective fields and communities.

4. Professional Development: The ZSPC provided opportunities for members to enhance their knowledge, skills, and competencies in sustainability through training sessions, webinars, and networking events. Professional development opportunities included certifications, internships, and mentorship programs with sustainability experts and practitioners.

5. Community Outreach: The ZSPC engaged in community outreach and advocacy efforts to promote the adoption of sustainability-driven principles beyond its membership. Awareness campaigns, educational workshops, and collaborative projects were organized to reach broader audiences and inspire positive change.

Outcomes and Benefits:

1. Mindset Shift: Members experienced a mindset shift towards sustainability, adopting values, attitudes, and behaviors aligned with the 12 Sustainability Driven Principles.

2. Behavioral Change: Individuals incorporated sustainable practices into their daily lives, workplaces, and communities, contributing to reduced environmental impact and improved quality of life.

3. Empowerment: Members felt empowered to take proactive steps towards sustainability leadership, innovation, and advocacy in their respective spheres of influence.

4. Collaboration and Networking: The ZSPC provided opportunities for members to connect, collaborate, and network with like-minded individuals and organizations, fostering a sense of belonging and solidarity within the sustainability community.
5. Community Impact: The collective efforts of ZSPC members led to tangible improvements in environmental stewardship, social inclusion, economic development, and governance at the local, regional, and global levels.
6. Leveraging Synergies: By aligning with the 12 Sustainability Driven Principles, the ZSPC leveraged synergies between environmental, social, and economic sustainability to create holistic and integrated solutions to complex sustainability challenges.

Thus, the ZHA Sustainability Practitioners Club successfully implemented sustainability-driven principles through its membership-based platform, engaging students, professionals, and common people in fostering a sustainability mindset. By integrating the 12 Sustainability Driven Principles into its activities and initiatives, the club facilitated a mindset shift towards sustainability.

Chapter 14:

ZHA Method of Integrating Sustainability into Students Education

The Role of Educational Institutions should be Promoting Sustainability Mindset Through Zha Sustainability Practitioners Club Integration:

Background:

With the growing recognition of the importance of sustainability in addressing global challenges, educational institutions are increasingly taking proactive measures to promote sustainability mindset among students. This case study highlights how a fictitious educational institution, Greenfield University, partnered with the ZHA Foundation to integrate sustainability principles into its curriculum through the ZHA Practitioners Club, aligning the next generation for sustainable lives.

Implementation:

Partnership Formation:

1. Greenfield University forged a partnership with the Zha Foundation to collaborate on sustainability initiatives. Together, they established the Zha Practitioners Club on campus, open to all students interested in sustainability.

Curriculum Integration:

2. The university integrated the ZHA Practitioners Club curriculum into its academic programs, offering sustainability-focused courses, workshops, and extracurricular activities. The curriculum, based on the ZHA Sustainability Mindset Framework, emphasized sustainability principles such as environmental stewardship, social responsibility, and economic resilience.

Club Activities:

3. The ZHA Practitioners Club at Greenfield University organized a variety of activities to engage students in sustainability education and action. These included sustainability workshops, guest lectures by industry experts, sustainability-themed competitions, and community service projects.

Student Participation:

4. Students actively participated in club activities, workshops, and events, gaining hands-on experience and practical skills in sustainability.

They collaborated on sustainability projects, conducted research on sustainability topics, and implemented initiatives to promote sustainability on campus and in the community.

Faculty Engagement:

5. Faculty members supported the integration of sustainability into the curriculum by incorporating sustainability principles into their teaching, research, and service activities. They mentored students, supervised sustainability projects, and contributed to interdisciplinary collaborations focused on sustainability.

Outcomes:

- ❖ Sustainability Mindset Adoption:
    - ➢ Students developed a deeper understanding of sustainability issues and solutions, embracing sustainability principles as core values in their personal and professional lives.

- Behavioral Change:
  - Students adopted sustainable behaviors, practices, and habits, reducing their ecological footprint and promoting environmental conservation, social equity, and economic prosperity.
- Leadership Development:
  - Students emerged as sustainability leaders, driving positive change on campus and in their communities through advocacy, activism, and innovative solutions to sustainability challenges.
- Institutional Impact:
  - Greenfield University became a model for sustainability education and action, inspiring other educational institutions to prioritize sustainability and integrate sustainability principles into their curricula and campus operations.
- Community Engagement:
  - The ZHA Practitioners Club at Greenfield University engaged with the local community, forging partnerships with businesses, NGOs, government agencies, and community organizations to address sustainability issues and promote sustainable development.

By integrating sustainability principles into its curriculum through the ZHA Practitioners Club integration, Greenfield University successfully promoted a sustainability mindset among students, aligning the next generation for sustainable lives. Through collaboration with the ZHA Foundation and active participation in club activities, students gained the knowledge, skills, and motivation to have a more sustainable future.

Case Study of Implementing the ZHA Sustainability Practitioners Club in Education Institutions:

Implementation:

1. Curriculum Development: The ZHA Foundation collaborated with sustainability experts, educators, and youth advocates to develop a comprehensive curriculum based on the ZHA Sustainability Mindset Framework. The curriculum incorporated interactive modules, case studies, and practical exercises to engage students in learning about sustainability principles and practices.

2. Club Formation: The ZSPC established partnership with colleges and schools, with student leaders appointed to lead the club activities. Membership was open to students interested in sustainability, with recruitment drives conducted at the beginning of each academic year.
3. Club Activities: The ZSPC organized a variety of activities, including workshops, seminars, field trips, and community projects, to engage members in sustainability education and action. Workshops covered topics such as sustainable consumption, renewable energy, waste management, and environmental conservation. Field trips provided hands-on learning experiences, such as visits to sustainable businesses, organic farms, and conservation sites.
4. Mentorship and Guidance: Experienced sustainability practitioners and educators served as mentors for club members, providing guidance, support, and expertise. Mentors facilitated discussions, offered advice on sustainability projects, and shared insights into career opportunities in the field of sustainability.
5. Partnerships and Collaborations: The ZSPC forged partnerships with local businesses, NGOs, government agencies, and community organizations to expand its impact and reach. Collaborative projects were undertaken to address specific sustainability challenges in the community, such as tree planting drives, clean-up campaigns, and awareness-raising events.

Outcomes:

1. Increased Awareness and Knowledge: Club members gained a deeper understanding of sustainability issues and solutions, as well as the interconnectedness of social, economic, and environmental systems.

2. Behavioral Change: Members adopted sustainable behaviors and practices in their daily lives, such as reducing waste, conserving energy, and supporting eco-friendly initiatives.

3. Empowerment and Leadership: Students developed leadership skills, confidence, and a sense of agency to drive positive change in their schools, communities, and beyond.

4. Community Impact: The ZSPC's projects and initiatives made tangible contributions to environmental conservation, social equity, and economic development in the local community.

5. Networking and Collaboration: Members benefited from networking opportunities, mentorship, and collaborations

with like-minded individuals and organizations, enhancing their professional and personal growth.

Conclusion:

The implementation of the ZHA Sustainability Practitioners Club initiative, guided by the ZHA Sustainability Mindset Framework, proved to be a successful model for engaging college and school students in sustainability education and action. By aligning club activities with the pillars of People, Prosperity, Planet, and Partnership, the initiative empowered students to become sustainability practitioners and change agents, contributing to a more sustainable and resilient future.

Chapter 15:

ZHA Maturity Framework for Sustainability Mindset

The ZHA Maturity Framework for Sustainability Mindset is designed to assess and benchmark the level of sustainability mindset among individuals and communities. It consists of four pillars, each representing key dimensions of sustainability mindset, and is tied to a curriculum that encompasses social work practices. Here's an outline of the framework:

Maturity Level 1: Awareness and Understanding

- Level 1: Basic Awareness - Individuals have limited knowledge of sustainability issues and their implications.
- Level 2: Intermediate Understanding - Individuals understand basic sustainability concepts but lack depth in understanding complex interconnections.

- Level 3: Advanced Awareness - Individuals have a comprehensive understanding of sustainability principles, including environmental, social, and economic dimensions.

Maturity Level 2: Values and Ethics

- Level 1: Compliance - Individuals adhere to sustainability practices due to external regulations or social pressure.
- Level 2: Engagement - Individuals embrace sustainability principles based on personal values and ethical considerations.
- Level 3: Advocacy - Individuals actively promote sustainability values and advocate for positive change in their communities and beyond.

Maturity Level 3: Action and Implementation

- Level 1: Passive Participation - Individuals passively engage in sustainability activities without taking proactive steps to drive change.
- Level 2: Proactive Engagement - Individuals take initiative to implement sustainable practices and initiatives in their personal and professional lives.
- Level 3: Leadership and Innovation - Individuals demonstrate leadership and innovation in advancing sustainability goals, inspiring others to follow suit.

Maturity Level 4: Collaboration and Partnership

- Level 1: Individual Efforts - Individuals work in isolation, lacking collaboration with others to address sustainability challenges.
- Level 2: Community Engagement - Individuals collaborate with peers, organizations, and stakeholders to leverage collective efforts for sustainability.

- Level 3: Global Citizenship - Individuals engage in cross-sectoral partnerships and international collaborations to address global sustainability issues comprehensively.

Curriculum Integration and Maturity Mapping:

The ZHA Maturity Framework for Sustainability Mindset is integrated into a comprehensive curriculum that encompasses social work practices. The curriculum includes modules and activities designed to develop awareness, values, actions, and collaboration related to sustainability mindset. It incorporates experiential learning, case studies, group projects, and real-world applications to enhance learning and engagement.

Benefits of the Framework:

1. Benchmarking Progress: The framework provides a structured approach to assess and benchmark the level of sustainability mindset among individuals and communities.
2. Identifying Gaps: It helps identify areas for improvement and gaps in sustainability knowledge, values, actions, and collaboration.
3. Guiding Development: The framework guides the development of tailored interventions, programs, and initiatives to enhance sustainability mindset at different levels.
4. Promoting Accountability: It fosters accountability for sustainability actions and outcomes among individuals and organizations.
5. Driving Collective Action: By emphasizing partnership, the framework encourages collective action and collaboration to address complex sustainability challenges comprehensively.

In conclusion, the ZHA Maturity Framework for Sustainability Mindset, tied to a curriculum encompassing social work practices, serves as a valuable tool for enabling individuals and communities to develop and enhance their sustainability mindset

Chapter 16:

Embracing the Circular Economy is the Key

ZHA Goal in Promoting Circular Economy through ZSPC

Enabling a sustainability mindset in students through our ZHA sustainability practitioner's curriculum and club can have profound impacts on circular economy practices. By educating students about sustainability principles, such as reducing waste and resource conservation, they become advocates for circular economy practices in their communities. This can lead to innovations in waste management, resource utilization, and product design, benefiting Tamil Nadu and India as a whole. A brief overview of how each pillar influences the circular economy:

1. Planet:

    ➢ Resource Conservation: A circular economy reduces reliance on finite resources by promoting practices such as recycling, remanufacturing, and reuse. This conserves natural resources such as minerals, water, and forests, reducing environmental degradation and habitat destruction.

    ➢ Waste Reduction: By minimizing waste generation and maximizing the value of materials throughout their lifecycle, a circular economy reduces the burden on landfills and incinerators. This mitigates pollution and greenhouse gas emissions associated with waste disposal, contributing to cleaner air, water, and soil.

2. People:

   - ➢ Job Creation: The transition to a circular economy creates opportunities for employment in industries such as recycling, repair, and re-manufacturing. This promotes economic inclusion and provides livelihoods for individuals across diverse skill sets and backgrounds.

   - ➢ Health and Well-being: A circular economy reduces exposure to harmful chemicals and pollutants associated with traditional linear production and consumption models. This improves public health outcomes, reduces healthcare costs, and enhances overall well-being for communities.

3. Partnership:

   - ➢ Collaboration Across Sectors: Transitioning to a circular economy requires collaboration and partnership among stakeholders across sectors, including government, businesses, academia, and civil society. This fosters innovation, knowledge sharing, and collective action to address complex sustainability challenges.

   - ➢ Supply Chain Resilience: Circular economy principles promote supply chain resilience by diversifying sourcing, reducing dependence on virgin materials, and minimizing supply chain disruptions. Partnerships across value chains enhance transparency, traceability, and accountability, driving sustainability and efficiency.

4. Prosperity:

   ➢ Economic Growth: A circular economy stimulates economic growth by creating new markets, business opportunities, and revenue streams. This fosters innovation, entrepreneurship, and investment in sustainable technologies and practices, driving job creation and economic prosperity.

   ➢ Resource Efficiency: By optimizing resource use and minimizing waste, a circular economy enhances productivity and efficiency across industries. This reduces production costs, increases competitiveness, and generates savings for businesses, contributing to long-term prosperity and competitiveness.

Integrating circular economy practices underscores its transformative potential to address environmental, social, and economic priorities while fostering collaboration and partnership across sectors. Through the ZHA sustainability practitioners curriculum and club, students can actively engage in projects and initiatives that promote circular economy practices, such as recycling programs, sustainable agriculture projects, and eco-friendly product development. These hands-on experiences not only reinforce classroom learning but also empower students to become leaders in sustainable development.

How partnerships can promote a circular economy?

Partnerships play a crucial role in promoting a circular economy by facilitating collaboration, knowledge sharing, and collective action among diverse stakeholders.

Here's how partnerships can promote a circular economy:

1. Cross-Sector Collaboration: Partnerships bring together stakeholders from various sectors, including government, businesses, academia, NGOs, and communities, to collaborate on circular economy initiatives. By leveraging the expertise, resources, and networks of different sectors, partnerships can drive innovation, scale up solutions, and address systemic barriers to circularity.

2. Knowledge Sharing and Capacity Building: Partnerships facilitate knowledge sharing and capacity building activities, such as workshops, training programs, and best practice exchanges, to enhance understanding of circular economy principles and practices among stakeholders. By

providing access to information, tools, and expertise, partnerships empower individuals and organizations to adopt circular business models, design sustainable products, and implement resource-efficient practices.

3. Technology and Innovation: Partnerships foster collaboration on research, development, and deployment of innovative technologies and solutions that enable circularity across value chains. By pooling resources and expertise, partners can accelerate the development and adoption of technologies such as recycling, re-manufacturing, and waste-to-resource processes, driving progress towards a circular economy.

4. Policy Advocacy and Regulation: Partnerships engage in policy advocacy and dialogue with policymakers to promote supportive regulatory frameworks and incentives for circular economy initiatives. By advocating for policies that prioritize resource efficiency, waste reduction, and sustainable consumption and production, creates an enabling environment for circularity and drive systemic change at the national and international levels.

5. Consumer Awareness and Engagement: Partnerships collaborate on public awareness campaigns, educational initiatives, and behavioral change programs to raise awareness of circular economy concepts and encourage sustainable consumption habits among consumers. By engaging with consumers through storytelling, social media, and interactive platforms, inspire behavior change and promote the adoption of circular lifestyle choices.

6. Circular Supply Chains: Partnerships work together to optimize supply chains and value networks for

circularity, fostering collaboration among suppliers, manufacturers, distributors, and retailers to redesign products, packaging, and logistics systems for resource efficiency and closed-loop solutions. By aligning incentives, sharing data, and coordinating efforts, partnerships drive the adoption of circular supply chain practices that minimize waste, reduce environmental impact, and create value for all stakeholders.

Overall, partnerships are essential for promoting a circular economy by fostering collaboration, knowledge sharing, and collective action among stakeholders. By working together across sectors and disciplines, partnerships can accelerate the transition to a circular economy, driving sustainable development, and creating shared value for society and the environment.

- **Partnership with Educational Institutions**

  Establish connections with schools and universities around the world to create a learning network. Through this network, students can participate in virtual exchange programs, collaborative international research projects, and global forums to discuss and solve key sustainability challenges.

- **Industry and Academic Collaborations:**

  Form partnerships with local businesses and industries to provide students with real-world experience through internships, apprenticeships, and joint research projects. This collaboration can also involve businesses sponsoring school projects related to sustainable development, providing both funding and expertise.

- **Community Partnerships:**

  Develop partnerships with local governments and non-governmental organizations (NGOs) to engage students in community-based projects. These projects can include urban sustainability initiatives, local environmental conservation efforts, and social outreach programs. This helps students apply their learning in real-world contexts and make a tangible impact in their communities.

- **Technology Sharing Initiatives:**

  Collaborate with tech companies to gain access to advanced technologies that can be used in educational settings. This can include software for simulating environmental changes, hardware for renewable energy projects, or platforms that facilitate remote learning and global classrooms.

- **Public Policy Engagement:**

  Encourage students to engage with policy-making processes through model United Nations programs or local government internships. This can help students understand the complexities of governance and public administration, particularly in relation to sustainability issues.

- **Funding and Resource Mobilization:**

  Work with external donors, alumni networks, and grant-making organizations to secure funding for sustainability projects. These funds can support the development of new sustainability courses, scholarships for research in sustainable development, or the creation of green spaces and sustainable facilities on campus.

Chapter 17:

How the curriculums in club promote a sustainability mindset among various communities, organizations and educational institutions:

Implementing Sustainability curriculum in schools and colleges. We carefully plan and execute a systematic strategy while instilling the sustainable mindset in students. We do not intend to boil the ocean by covering every facet of ESG(Environmental, Social, and Governance), but we have designed a curriculum that will be easily comprehended by students at their level, as well as how they can practice in particular and contribute to society in general.

Define objectives: By outlining the Sustainability curriculum's endeavors and goals, as well as the values and virtues that will be taught to students. Empathy, honesty, integrity, respect, and responsibility are some examples.

Curriculum Development: The Zha Practitioners Club offers a complete curriculum that includes both theoretical and practical chapters. The curriculum is age-appropriate and includes a variety of themes relevant to students' lives. The curriculum will be regularly improved based on input from the field and knowledge gained in the practitioners club.

1. **Teacher Training:**

   While Zha Club will offer Governors to operate the program in schools and colleges, we will also provide teachers with training and content to have the required skills and knowledge. Their buy-in is necessary to ensure the program's success. Teachers should grasp the value of sustainability education and be able to organize relevant classroom discussions and activities.

- Role-playing, group discussions, case studies, storytelling, and experiential learning activities will be part of the curriculum which are all effective ways to engage students and stimulate critical thinking about sustainability concerns.

- Incorporate Real-Life Examples: Use real-life examples and scenarios that illustrate principles and inspire students to use them in their daily lives. This makes the learning experience more meaningful and relatable for pupils.

- Encourage Ethical Decision Making: Teach students how to make ethical judgments by exploring moral dilemmas and encouraging them to evaluate the impact of their actions on themselves and others.

2. **Encourage Reflection and Discussion:** The curricular encourages students to reflect on their own values and beliefs while engaging in open and polite discussions with their peers. Encourage students to investigate, analyze, and assess sustainability concerns from a variety of angles. (For example, prohibiting plastics will have a significant influence on those who rely on the plastic industry, how to look at challenges in their shoes and what can be the best approach for achieving balance).

3. **Parental Involvement:** Include parents and guardians in the sustainability education process by keeping them up to date on the curriculum and encouraging them to reinforce sustainable practices at home.

4. **Assessment and Evaluation:** Create acceptable techniques for evaluating students' sustainability progress, such as essays, presentations, projects, and self-assessments. Evaluation should include not only information acquisition but also the application of ideas in real-world settings.

5. **Continuous Improvement:** Evaluate the sustainability curriculum's success on a regular basis and make required changes based on teachers, students, and parents feedback. Continuously seek to improve and enhance the curriculum in order to better fulfill the needs of the pupils.

Success stories from the curriculum of our ZSPC

One success story from the curriculum of the Zha Sustainability Practitioners Club (ZSPC) involves a group of students from a renowned arts and science college who participated in a sustainability project focused on waste management and recycling.

Here's a detailed account of their success story:

Background:

The arts and science college, known for its commitment to sustainability and innovation, established a ZSPC chapter to engage students in practical sustainability initiatives. The club's curriculum integrated lessons from the Zha Framework for Sustainability Mindset, focusing on the pillars of planet, people, prosperity, and partnership.

Project Overview:

The project undertaken by the ZSPC students aimed to address the issue of waste management on campus and promote recycling practices among students and faculty. The project involved several stages, including research, planning, implementation, and evaluation.

Research and Planning:

The students conducted a thorough assessment of the college's waste generation patterns, identifying key sources of waste and areas for improvement. They researched best practices in waste management and recycling, seeking inspiration from successful initiatives implemented in other educational institutions.

Implementation:

Based on their research findings, the students developed a comprehensive waste management plan tailored to the college's needs and resources. They established designated recycling bins across campus, organized awareness campaigns to educate students and faculty about proper waste sorting and recycling techniques, and collaborated with local recycling facilities to ensure the proper disposal and recycling of collected materials.

Community Engagement:

The students actively engaged the college community in their sustainability efforts, organizing workshops, seminars, and hands-on activities to raise awareness and promote behavior change. They encouraged students and faculty to participate in waste sorting and recycling initiatives, fostering a culture of environmental responsibility and collective action.

Evaluation and Impact:

Throughout the project, the students conducted regular evaluations to assess the effectiveness of their interventions and measure their impact on waste reduction and recycling rates. They collected data on the volume of waste diverted from landfills, the number of recycling bins used, and the level of participation in recycling activities.

Outcome : Successes and Achievements

- Increased Awareness: The project successfully raised awareness about waste management and recycling among students and faculty, leading to improved waste sorting behaviors and increased participation in recycling initiatives.
- Waste Reduction: By implementing effective waste management strategies and promoting recycling practices, the students were able to significantly reduce the college's overall waste output, diverting a considerable amount of materials from landfills.
- Sustainable Behavior Change: The project instilled a sense of environmental stewardship and responsibility among the college community, fostering sustainable behaviors and habits that extended beyond the duration of the project.

- Recognition and Awards: The students' efforts were recognized and celebrated both within the college and in the wider community, earning them the accolades and awards for their outstanding contributions to sustainability.

Conclusion:

Through their participation in the ZSPC curriculum, the students from the arts and science college demonstrated the transformative power of sustainability education and hands-on experience. Their success story serves as an inspiring example of how students can drive positive change and make a meaningful impact on their campus and beyond through collaborative and innovative sustainability initiatives.

Chapter 18:

Looking Ahead & Target State

The future of ZHA sustainability practitioners club which promotes the circular economy

The story of the Zha Foundation begins with successful professionals across various industries who desired to contribute to the global development of sustainable living. However, they found a lack of innovative platforms aligning with their values. Simultaneously, successful businessmen had exclusive business clubs that instilled pride in their achievements.

Recognizing this gap, the founder of Zha believed in the necessity of forming a strategic social work board. This board would consist of accomplished professionals and business leaders at all levels and from diverse locations. The aim was to propagate the Zha sustainability movement, raising awareness among the general public and fostering a global impact.

The founder of Zha envisioned the creation of a purposeful hobby benefiting the planet and everyone's well-being, inspired by the caring and sharing model embedded in sustainability principles. Thus, the overarching theme of Zha Foundation became sustainability.

The role of the next generation in promoting sustainability for the outcomes:

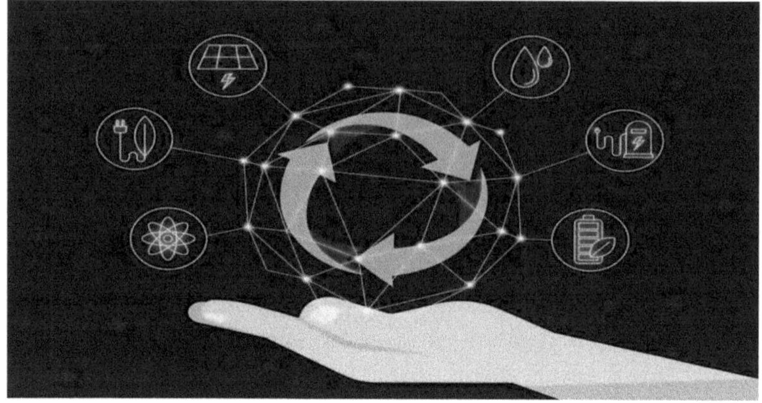

- **Individual Empowerment :** Through Zha's sustainability programs, common individuals, women, men, and students are empowered to adopt a sustainable mindset. The foundation's focus on inclusivity ensures that everyone can contribute to the betterment of the planet.
- **Global Impact :** By aligning with the United Nations' sustainable goals and ESG measurements, Zha Foundation contributes to global initiatives for sustainable development. The benchmark theory of sustainability, applicable to individuals worldwide, emphasizes a collective effort towards positive change.
- **Measurable Impact :** Zha's methodology provides a tangible way for individuals to measure their sustainability mindset capabilities. This allows people to track and understand their contributions to sustainable living.

- **Education and Awareness :** Zha Foundation leverages technology and tools to offer free resources, fostering public understanding of the United Nations' sustainability goals. This educational aspect promotes awareness and encourages a broader adoption of sustainable practices.
- **Comprehensive Framework :** The Zha sustainability enabler framework, with its key practice areas, provides a structured and comprehensive approach to sustainable living. This framework guides individuals incorporating sustainability into various aspects of their lives.
- **Community Building :** The caring and sharing model embedded in sustainability principles fosters a sense of community and collective responsibility. Zha Foundation encourages individuals to collaborate, creating a network of like-minded people dedicated to sustainable practices.

Final thoughts and call to action

Zha Foundation is committed to establishing a benchmark theory of sustainability applicable to all individuals, not just corporations. In alignment with the United Nations' sustainable goals and ESG measurements, Zha has developed a methodology tailored for the general public.

The Zha sustainability programs aim to empower the public, including common individuals, women, men, and students, to embrace the principles and values of the Zha sustainability enabler framework. This framework serves as a methodology for all humans to adopt, allowing them to measure their sustainability mindset capabilities. Leveraging technology and tools, Zha Foundation provides free resources to help the public understand the United Nations' sustainability goals. The methodology includes key practice areas within the Zha sustainability enabler framework, shaping a comprehensive approach to sustainable living.

Proposed Interventions

The Zha Sustainability Practitioners Curriculum encompasses a comprehensive solution in line with the Tamil Nadu government's aim for preservation of the environment and sustainable development. We propose a phased implementation strategy that covers all 38 districts in Tamil Nadu, with four schools and institutions in each district.

The Zha Sustainability Practitioners Curriculum takes a multifaceted approach to addressing these issues by:

Fostering Environmental Literacy: Providing students with a deep understanding of environmental issues, their root causes, and potential solutions.

Promoting Sustainable Practices: Equipping students with the knowledge and skills to adopt sustainable practices in their daily lives, such as reducing energy consumption, conserving water, minimizing waste, and making responsible consumer choices.

Encouraging Active Citizenship: Empowering students to become advocates for sustainability, engaging in community initiatives, and influencing policy changes.

Developing Green Skills: Cultivating skills and knowledge relevant to green careers, preparing students for future employment opportunities in sustainability-related fields.

Chapter 19:

How do we engage students practically in ZSPC sustainability initiatives?

Engaging students practically in sustainability initiatives can be a transformative experience. Here are some strategies:

1. Hands-On Projects: Encourage students to participate in projects that have a real-world impact. This could include setting up a recycling program at school, starting a community garden, or organizing a local clean-up event.

2. Field Trips: Organize visits to local businesses or organizations that are known for their sustainability practices. This could provide students with a first-hand look at how sustainability can be implemented in a practical setting.

3. Guest Speakers: Invite professionals who work in the field of sustainability to speak to students. They can share their experiences and provide insights into how sustainability is applied in their profession.

4. Sustainability Challenges: Organize challenges or competitions that encourage students to come up with innovative solutions to sustainability problems. This could range from designing an energy-efficient building to come up with a business plan for a sustainable enterprise.

5. Curriculum Integration: Incorporate sustainability into the existing curriculum. For example, in a science class, students could learn about renewable energy sources. In a social studies class, they could explore the social and economic aspects of sustainability.

6. Student-Led Initiatives: Encourage students to take the lead in sustainability initiatives. This could involve setting up a sustainability club, organizing awareness campaigns, or advocating for sustainable practices within the school.

7. Community Service: Encourage students to participate in community service activities that promote sustainability. This could include tree planting, beach clean-ups, or volunteering at a local recycling center.

8. Sustainability in Daily Life: Encourage students to practice sustainability in their daily lives. This could include reducing waste, conserving water and energy, and making sustainable food choices.

Remember, the goal is not just to teach students about sustainability, but to empower them to become active participants in creating a more sustainable future.

How can we measure the impact of these ZSPC initiatives?

Measuring the impact of sustainability initiatives can be done through both qualitative and quantitative methods. Here are some ways to do it:

1. Surveys and Feedback: Conduct surveys among students and staff to gauge their awareness and attitudes towards sustainability before and after the initiatives. This can help measure changes in knowledge, attitudes, and behaviors.

2. Observation: Monitor the school environment and observe changes. For example, if a recycling program was implemented, is there a noticeable reduction in waste? If a garden was planted, has biodiversity increased?

3. Data Collection: Collect data on key indicators related to the initiatives. This could include the amount of waste generated and recycled, energy consumption, water usage, etc. Comparing these figures before and after the initiatives can provide a quantitative measure of impact.

4. Participation Rates: Track the number of students participating in sustainability initiatives. High participation rates can indicate a high level of engagement and interest in sustainability.
5. Sustainability Reporting: Develop a sustainability report that documents all the sustainability initiatives undertaken and their impacts. This can provide a comprehensive overview of the school's sustainability efforts and their outcomes.
6. External Recognition: Apply for sustainability awards or certifications. Recognition from external bodies can provide validation of the effectiveness of the sustainability initiatives.
7. Long-Term Impact: Track graduates and see how many are pursuing careers or lifestyles that align with sustainability. This can provide a measure of the long-term impact of the initiatives.

Remember, the goal of these initiatives is not just to reduce environmental impact, but also to instill a sustainability mindset in students. Therefore, the true impact might be seen years down the line, as students apply what they've learned to their lives and careers.

Examples of student-led sustainability projects?

1. **Waste Management Campaign**: Students can initiate a campaign to reduce waste in their school. This could involve setting up recycling stations, promoting composting of organic waste, and educating others about the importance of reducing, reusing, and recycling.
2. **Energy Conservation Initiative**: Students can lead an initiative to reduce energy consumption in the school. This could include conducting energy audits, promoting energy-efficient practices, and advocating for the use of renewable energy sources.
3. **Sustainable Gardening Project**: Students can create a school garden using sustainable gardening practices. This could involve growing organic vegetables, creating a compost pile, and even setting up a rainwater harvesting system.

4. **Green Transport Campaign**: Students can promote sustainable transportation methods. This could involve organizing carpooling groups, encouraging walking or cycling to school, and advocating for public transportation.
5. **Conservation Club**: Students can start a club dedicated to conservation efforts. The club could organize tree planting events, clean-up drives, and awareness campaigns about local environmental issues.
6. **Sustainable Art Projects**: Students can use art to promote sustainability. This could involve creating art from recycled materials, organizing exhibitions on environmental themes, or using art to raise awareness about sustainability issues.
7. **Community Outreach Programs**: Students can organize events to educate the local community about sustainability. This could involve hosting workshops, giving presentations, or creating educational materials about sustainability.
8. **Research Projects**: Older students can conduct research on sustainability topics. This could involve studying local ecosystems, researching renewable energy options, or investigating the impact of certain practices on the environment.

Remember, the goal of these projects is not just to make a positive environmental impact, but also to develop leadership skills, foster teamwork, and instill a lifelong commitment to sustainability in students.

Chapter 20:

Recommendation by ZSPC to the global partners:

Recommending companies, educational institutions, government organizations, and corporates to adopt the ZHA methodology for fostering a sustainability mindset can lead to significant benefits, especially through global alignment in sustainable practices. Here's how the ZHA methodology can be effectively recommended and the potential benefits of its implementation:

Idea behind the ZHA Methodology:

For Companies:

1. Integrate Sustainability into Corporate Culture:
    - Embed sustainability principles into the company's core values and operational strategies.
    - Conduct regular training programs to educate employees about sustainable practices and their importance.
2. Adopt Sustainable Business Practices:
    - Implement eco-friendly production processes and sustainable supply chain management.
    - Focus on energy efficiency, waste reduction, and the use of renewable resources.

For Educational Institutions:

1. Incorporate Sustainability in the Curriculum:
    - Develop and integrate sustainability-focused courses and modules across various disciplines.
    - Encourage interdisciplinary projects and research on sustainability topics.
2. Promote Campus Sustainability Initiatives:
    - Implement recycling programs, energy-saving measures, and sustainable transportation options.
    - Foster a culture of sustainability through student-led initiatives and sustainability clubs.

For Government Organizations:

1. Develop and Enforce Sustainability Policies:
    - Formulate policies that promote sustainable development and environmental protection.
    - Ensure compliance with international sustainability standards and guidelines.
2. Lead by Example:
    - Implement sustainable practices within government operations and facilities.
    - Support community sustainability projects and public awareness campaigns.

For Corporates:

1. Align Corporate Strategies with Sustainability Goals:
    - Integrate sustainability into corporate governance and strategic planning.
    - Report on sustainability performance and set measurable sustainability targets.
2. Engage Stakeholders in Sustainability Efforts:

- Collaborate with suppliers, customers, and partners to promote sustainable practices.
- Invest in sustainability-focused innovation and technologies.

Benefits of Global Alignment Through the ZHA Methodology:

1. Enhanced Reputation and Brand Value:

Demonstrating a commitment to sustainability can enhance the reputation and brand value of organizations, attracting customers, investors, and talent.

2. Operational Efficiency and Cost Savings:

Sustainable practices often lead to increased efficiency and reduced operational costs through energy savings, waste reduction, and resource optimization.

3. Compliance and Risk Management:

Aligning with global sustainability standards helps organizations stay compliant with regulations and manage risks associated with environmental and social issues.

4. Market Competitiveness:

Companies and organizations that adopt sustainable practices can gain a competitive edge in the market by meeting the growing demand for eco-friendly products and services.

5. Positive Environmental Impact:

The widespread adoption of the ZHA methodology can lead to significant environmental benefits, including reduced carbon footprint, conservation of natural resources, and biodiversity protection.

6. Social and Community Benefits:

Promoting sustainability can enhance community well-being by creating healthier environments, supporting local economies, and improving quality of life.

7. Innovation and Growth:

Focusing on sustainability can drive innovation, leading to the development of new products, services, and business models that contribute to long-term growth and resilience.

8. Global Collaboration and Knowledge Sharing:

Adoption of the ZHA methodology encourages global collaboration and the sharing of best practices, fostering a collective effort towards achieving sustainability goals.

By recommending and adopting the ZHA methodology, companies, educational institutions, government organizations, and corporates can not only improve their own sustainability practices but also contribute to a globally aligned effort towards a more sustainable future.

Chapter 21:

ZSPC Membership Program Overview

The ZSPC is a Path for communities across globe who can be part of the club activities via Membership Program and it offers various tiers of membership tailored to different groups, providing access to resources, educational materials, and opportunities to engage in sustainability initiatives. Each membership tier is designed to meet the specific needs and goals of its members, fostering a community dedicated to sustainable development.

Basic Membership

Cost: 300 rupees per month

Description: The Basic Membership is designed for individuals looking to incorporate sustainability into their everyday lives.

Benefits:

- Access to Essential Resources: Members receive materials that provide guidance on sustainable practices.
- Community Discussions: Participate in forums and discussions with like-minded individuals to share ideas and experiences.
- Regular Updates: Stay informed with the latest sustainability news and best practices.

Student Membership

Cost: 100 rupees per month or 1000 rupees annually

Description: Tailored for students eager to learn about and contribute to sustainability efforts, this membership connects students with resources and peers.

Benefits:

- Educational Resources: Access to learning materials that deepen understanding of sustainability.
- Mentorship Programs: Guidance from experienced professionals in the field.
- Student-led Initiatives: Opportunities to engage in projects and initiatives, gaining hands-on experience.

Professionals Board Membership

Cost: 600 rupees per month

Description: This membership is for professionals aiming to integrate sustainability in their careers and industries.

Benefits:

- Advanced Workshops: Participate in specialized training sessions to enhance skills.
- Industry Insights: Access to exclusive information on the latest trends in sustainability.
- Collaborative Projects: Work alongside seasoned practitioners on impactful projects.

Strategic Board Membership

Cost: 1000 rupees per month

Description: Designed for leaders driving significant change in their organizations or communities.

Benefits:

- Strategic Planning Sessions: Engage in high-level planning to implement effective sustainability initiatives.
- Executive Forums: Access to forums with other leaders for networking and idea exchange.

- Personalized Guidance: Receive tailored advice on maximizing sustainability impact.

NRI Board Membership

Cost: 10,000 rupees annually

Description: For non-resident Indians dedicated to supporting sustainability efforts in India.

Benefits:

- Virtual Networking: Opportunities to connect with other NRIs and stakeholders virtually.
- Online Resources: Access comprehensive digital resources from anywhere in the world.
- Commitment to India: Demonstrate support for sustainable development in India, contributing to its progress from afar.

Benefits of the ZSPC Membership Program

1. Personal Growth and Education:
    - Access to a wealth of resources and educational materials helps members grow their knowledge and skills in sustainability.
    - Mentorship programs and workshops offer personal development opportunities.
    - Professional Development:
    - Specialized training and industry insights help professionals stay ahead in their careers.
    - Networking events and collaborative projects foster valuable connections and partnerships.

2. Community Engagement:
    - Members can participate in discussions and initiatives, fostering a sense of community and shared purpose
    - Engaging in student-led projects or professional collaborations promotes active participation in sustainability efforts.

3. Strategic Impact:
    - Leaders and professionals receive strategic guidance and support to implement impactful sustainability initiatives.
    - Executive forums and high-level networking events provide platforms for sharing ideas and strategies.
4. Global Alignment:
    - The program supports global sustainability goals by aligning local efforts with international standards and practices.
    - NRI members contribute to sustainable development in India, fostering global collaboration and support.
5. Cost-Effective Access:
    - Affordable membership fees ensure accessibility for individuals, students, and professionals, making sustainability resources widely available.

The membership model of the ZHA Sustainability Practitioners Club offers various levels of Reward and Recognition:

By joining the ZSPC Membership Program, members not only enhance their understanding and practice of sustainability but also contribute to a larger movement towards a sustainable future. Each membership tier offers unique benefits tailored to different needs, ensuring that everyone can play a part in driving sustainable change.

Platinum Level Society Development Contributor

This tier represents the highest level of commitment and contribution to societal development through sustainability initiatives.

Membership Fee: Typically higher than other levels, reflecting the significant support provided.

Benefits:

- VIP Access to Events: Exclusive entry to major events, conferences, and workshops.
- Personalized Consultations: One-on-one sessions with sustainability experts to tailor strategies and initiatives.
- Recognition: Acknowledgment as leaders in the field, with opportunities for public recognition and awards

Gold Level Society Development Contributor

Gold-level members are recognized for their significant contributions to sustainability efforts.

Benefits:

- Priority Registration: Early access to register for popular workshops and seminars.
- Networking Opportunities: Chances to connect with industry leaders and key stakeholders in sustainability.
- Premium Educational Resources: Access to advanced materials and resources on sustainability practices.

Silver Level Society Development Contributor

Silver-level members are valued contributors to sustainability initiatives.

Benefits:

- Discounted Rates: Reduced fees for events and training programs.
- Online Forums and Discussion Groups: Access to exclusive online communities for exchanging ideas and experiences.
- Regular Updates: Receive the latest information on sustainability trends and developments.

Bronze Level Society Development Contributor

Bronze-level members are essential supporters of sustainability efforts.

Benefits:

- Curated Content and Resources: Access to specially selected materials on sustainability topics.
- Local Networking Events: Invitations to events in their area to connect with other sustainability enthusiasts.
- Recognition: Acknowledgment for their contributions, which may include mentions in newsletters or on the organization's website.

Allocation of Membership Fees for ZSPC Activities

The membership fees collected from the ZSPC Membership Program are strategically utilized to support various aspects of the organization's operations and initiatives.

Here's a breakdown of how the funds are typically allocated:

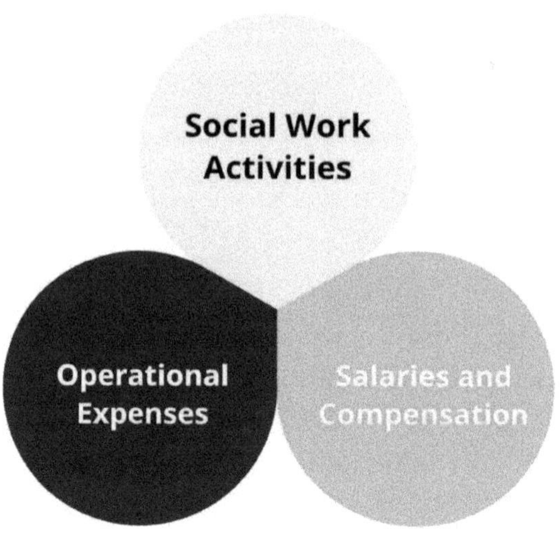

1. Social Work Activities:

    - Community Projects: A portion of the fees supports local and regional sustainability projects aimed at improving community infrastructure, promoting green practices, and enhancing public awareness about sustainability.
    - Educational Outreach: Funding is used to develop and distribute educational materials, conduct workshops and seminars, and support school and community-based sustainability programs.
    - Environmental Conservation: Fees contribute to conservation efforts such as tree planting, waste management programs, and water conservation initiatives.

2. Operational Expenses:

    - Administrative Costs: Covering day-to-day expenses to keep the ZSPC functioning smoothly, including office supplies, utilities, and communication costs.

- Event Management: Organizing events such as workshops, seminars, and conferences that require venue rentals, equipment, and logistical support.

- Technology and Infrastructure: Maintaining the digital platforms and necessary tools for managing memberships, providing online resources, and facilitating virtual events and discussions.

3. Salaries and Compensation:

    - Staff Salaries: Paying the salaries of the administrative and support staff who handle the operations, manage programs, and ensure the smooth running of ZSPC activities.

    - Expert Fees: Compensating sustainability experts, trainers, and consultants who provide specialized knowledge, conduct training sessions, and offer personalized consultations to members.

Impact of Membership Contributions

By contributing to the ZSPC through various membership levels, members not only gain access to valuable resources and networks but also play a crucial role in advancing sustainability initiatives. Their financial support enables the organization to:

- Expand Educational Programs: More resources can be developed and distributed, reaching a wider audience and increasing sustainability awareness.

- Enhance Community Impact: Greater funding allows for more extensive community projects and environmental conservation efforts.
- Sustain Operations: Reliable income helps maintain the operational infrastructure, ensuring the continuity and effectiveness of ZSPC activities.
- Attract and Retain Talent: Adequate compensation for staff and experts ensures that the organization can attract and retain knowledgeable and dedicated individuals.

Overall, the structured allocation of membership fees ensures that the ZSPC can fulfill its mission of promoting sustainability and making a tangible impact on both local and global scales.

Chapter 22:

ZSPC Sustainable Social Work Offerings

Farmers Transformation Program: "Organic Farmers League"

Objective: To promote sustainable agriculture and improve the livelihoods of farmers.

Activities:

- Training farmers in organic farming techniques to enhance soil health and reduce chemical usage.
- Providing resources and support to farmers for transitioning to organic farming.

- Facilitating a network of organic farmers to share knowledge and market their produce.
- Impact: Improved farm productivity, healthier food products, reduced environmental impact, and better economic stability for farmers.

Tree Plantation

Objective: To combat deforestation and enhance green cover.

Activities:

- Organizing tree planting drives in urban, suburban, and rural areas.
- Engaging community members, including students and local residents, in planting and caring for trees.

- Partnering with local authorities and environmental organizations to ensure sustainability.
- Impact: Increased green cover, improved air quality, enhanced biodiversity, and community engagement in environmental conservation.

Youth Mind Wellness Marathon for Rural Children

Objective: To promote mental health and well-being among rural youth.

Activities:

- Conducting workshops and activities focused on mindfulness, stress management, and emotional well-being.
- Providing access to mental health resources and counseling services.
- Organizing recreational and physical activities to foster holistic development.
- Impact: Enhanced mental health awareness, reduced stress levels, and improved overall well-being of rural children.

Women Empowerment: Free Study Centre for Higher Studies and Skill Development Centre

Objective: To empower women through education and skill development.

Activities:

- Establishing study centers that provide free tutoring and resources for higher education.
- Offering vocational training and skill development programs tailored for local needs.
- Facilitating mentorship and support networks for women to pursue their career and educational goals.
- Impact: Increased educational attainment, improved employability, economic independence, and empowerment of women.

Disaster Fix Volunteers

Objective: To prepare and support communities in disaster response and recovery.

Activities:

- Training volunteers in disaster preparedness, response, and recovery techniques.
- Creating rapid response teams to assist in disaster-affected areas.
- Coordinating with local authorities and NGOs for efficient disaster management.
- Impact: Enhanced community resilience, quicker recovery from disasters, and reduced loss of life and property.

Environment Cleanliness: Beach Cleaning and Campus Cleaning

Objective: To promote environmental cleanliness and community involvement.

Activities:

- Organizing regular beach and campus cleaning drives to remove litter and pollutants.
- Educating participants on the importance of waste management and recycling.
- Collaborating with local governments and environmental organizations to sustain cleanliness efforts.
- Impact: Cleaner environments, reduced pollution, heightened environmental awareness, and community participation in conservation efforts.

Real Estate, Manufacturing Sectors, Other Industries and Eco-Friendly

Certification Programs

Objective: To promote sustainability in real estate and manufacturing industries.

Activities:

- Developing and implementing eco-friendly certification standards for buildings and manufacturing processes.
- Conducting audits and assessments to ensure compliance with sustainability criteria.
- Providing training and resources to industry stakeholders on sustainable practices.
- Impact: Reduced environmental footprint of industries, enhanced sustainability practices, and recognition of eco-friendly initiatives.

ZHA Recognition Award for Rural, Suburban and Corporate Employees and

General Public

Objective: To acknowledge and reward efforts in sustainability and social responsibility.

Activities:

- Identifying individuals and organizations that demonstrate exceptional commitment to sustainability.
- Organizing award ceremonies to celebrate achievements and share best practices.
- Promoting awardees as role models to inspire others.
- Impact: Increased motivation to adopt sustainable practices, public recognition of efforts, and promotion of sustainability role models.

Free Sports and Physical Wellness Training for Rural and Suburban Children Objective: To promote physical health and well-being among children.

Activities:

- Offering free sports training programs and physical wellness activities.
- Providing access to sports facilities and equipment.
- Encouraging participation in regular physical activity to foster healthy lifestyles.
- Impact: Improved physical fitness, enhanced social skills, and better overall health of rural and suburban children.

Summary

These social work offerings by ZSPC not only empower individuals and communities to adopt sustainable practices but also foster a culture of social responsibility, environmental stewardship, and personal growth. By engaging diverse groups in meaningful activities, ZSPC aims to create more sustainable, equitable, and resilient society.

Chapter 23:

ZHA Methodology for Sustainability Mindset is dedicated to Next Generations:

The ZHA Methodology for Sustainability Mindset is an innovative framework developed to instill a deep sense of environmental responsibility and sustainability consciousness in individuals, particularly focusing on the younger generation. It aims to create a holistic understanding of sustainability, encompassing ecological, economic, and social dimensions, to ensure that future generations are equipped to face the challenges of a changing world.

Core Principles

Holistic Education: The ZHA Methodology emphasizes an interdisciplinary approach to sustainability education, integrating knowledge from science, economics, sociology, and ethics. This ensures a comprehensive understanding of sustainability issues.

Active Engagement: Encouraging active participation and hands-on experiences, the methodology involves students in real-world projects and community-based initiatives. This practical approach helps solidify theoretical knowledge through tangible actions.

Critical Thinking and Innovation: Developing critical thinking skills and fostering innovation are central to the methodology. It encourages students to question existing practices, think creatively, and develop sustainable solutions to contemporary problems.

Global and Local Perspectives: The methodology balances global sustainability issues with local context. It highlights the interconnectedness of global systems while encouraging students to take actionable steps within their own communities.

Ethical Responsibility: Ethical considerations are integral to the ZHA Methodology. It instills a sense of moral responsibility towards the environment and future generations, promoting values such as equity, justice, and stewardship.

Implementation Strategies

Curriculum Integration: The ZHA Methodology is integrated into the existing curriculum across various subjects. By embedding sustainability concepts into subjects like science, geography, economics, and civics, it ensures that sustainability becomes a core part of the educational experience.

Project-Based Learning: Students engage in project-based learning activities that address real-world sustainability challenges. These projects often involve collaboration with local communities, businesses, and government agencies, providing students with practical insights and experiences.

Workshops and Seminars: Regular workshops and seminars conducted by experts in sustainability help keep students and educators informed about the latest trends and developments. These sessions provide a platform for sharing knowledge, experiences, and best practices.

Sustainability Clubs and Initiatives: Establishing sustainability clubs within schools and colleges encourages peer learning and leadership. These clubs organize various activities such as recycling drives, energy conservation campaigns, and awareness programs, fostering a culture of sustainability.

Mentorship and Support: Providing mentorship and support from sustainability professionals helps guide students in their projects and initiatives. Mentors offer valuable advice, resources, and connections, aiding students in achieving their sustainability goals.

Impact on Next Generations

The ZHA Methodology is dedicated to nurturing a sustainability mindset in the next generation. By instilling the values of sustainability at an early age, it aims to:

Empower Youth: Equip young people with the knowledge, skills, and confidence to address environmental challenges and advocate for sustainable practices.

Foster Leadership: Cultivate future leaders who are committed to sustainability and capable of driving change in their communities and beyond.

Promote Lifelong Learning: Encourage a lifelong commitment to learning and adapting to new sustainability practices and technologies.

Enhance Community Resilience: Strengthen community resilience by promoting local sustainability initiatives and fostering a collaborative approach to problem-solving.

Conclusion

The ZHA Methodology for Sustainability Mindset is a comprehensive approach designed to prepare the next generations for a sustainable future via ZSPC. By integrating sustainability into education through club practices and promoting active engagement, critical thinking, and ethical responsibility, it aims to create a generation of informed, responsible, and proactive citizens. Through this methodology, the commitment to sustainability becomes not just a part of the curriculum but a fundamental aspect of life, ensuring a brighter, more sustainable future for all.

www.ingramcontent.com/pod-product-compliance
Lightning Source LLC
LaVergne TN
LVHW070843160826
845684LV00008B/63

* 9 7 9 8 8 9 4 9 8 0 5 8 4 *